Digitally Remastered

ISBN 978-1-5310-2694-3
eISBN 978-1-5310-2695-0

See catalog.loc.gov for
Library of Congress Cataloging-in-Publication Data.

Carolina Academic Press
700 Kent Street
Durham, NC 27701
(919) 489-7486
www.cap-press.com

Printed in the United States of America

Digitally Remastered

Modern Law School

Jessica Carmichael

Bethany Carr

Sarah Covington

CAROLINA ACADEMIC PRESS

Durham, North Carolina

Our families, for the love and support
Lisa Blasser, for the encouragement on the business side
Kendra Brown, for the inspiration to not give up

Contents

Section One: Introduction

Section One

Introduction

▷▷▷ 1

What Is That Word?

This is a glossary of legal industry terms you may run into throughout your law school experience. If you are reading a case and run into terms you do not know, look them up in a legal dictionary (either a hard copy or online). The terms you will find here are the terms that traditional residential 1Ls learn through their daily interactions in the law school, whether it be with students, professors, or even flyers on the wall.

Rather than ending on the glossary, we encourage you to start with it. We know it's more common to have it in the back of a book, but we firmly believe that having a grasp on the following terms, words, and processes will help make your experience a smoother one.

1L: First year law student. A law student in a non-traditional program that lasts longer than 3 years will be considered a 1L until they have completed 1/3 of the program's required credits.

2L: Second year law student. A law student in a non-traditional program that lasts longer than 3 years will be considered a 2L once they have completed 1/3 of the program's required credits, but have not reached 2/3 of the required credits.

3L: Third year law students. A law student in a non-traditional program that lasts longer than 3 years will be considered a 3L once they have completed 2/3 of the program's required credits.

ABA: American Bar Association. A national organization of legal professionals that has many functions, including promoting continuing education, sharing news, and advocating for the legal profession. The organization also has specially focused groups based on geography, tenure, and practice area.

Accommodations: These are intentional steps or processes taken to ensure your success in law school. They may be legally required, or just granted as needed. See Chapter 5 for more specifics.

ADR: Alternative Dispute Resolution. A method of resolving a case without litigation. This is generally mediation or arbitration.

Appellant: The party appealing the lower court's decision. The appellant may also be called the petitioner.

Appellee: The party who initially won the case at the lower court and is arguing to keep the lower court's decision when the case is appealed. The appellee may also be called the respondent.

Asynch: Course content that is done without any live interaction. It may include lecture videos, quiz-like modules, and discussion posts. See Chapter 2 for more specifics.

Attack Outline: Your attack outline will be a one to two page document that captures the key points from the semester. It will not have every piece of information you have learned, just the key information necessary to jog your memory.

Bar: An association of attorneys. There is a national bar association (the ABA). Each state has a bar association that is generally overseen by the state's supreme court. Districts, counties, and towns may also have a bar association.

Bar Exam: The exam to become a lawyer. States are able to create their own exam, or use all or part of the UBE (Uniform Bar Exam). The bar exam is offered twice a year, in February and July. By the time you take the bar exam, the NextGen bar exam will have replaced the UBE.

Barbri: A study resource that gives access to practice materials. It is especially well known for its MPRE and bar prep resources. This resource has helpful 1L outlines, as well as practice problems.

Barrister's Ball: A formal event held by law schools that is similar to the idea of prom. It is often organized by the SBA and faculty members attend. There may be awards and superlatives given out during the event.

Big Law: The largest law firms, typically with over one thousand attorneys and the revenue to prove it (sometimes written as Biglaw).

Black Letter Law: Black letter law is the doctrinal rule or rules that are drawn from a case. For more details regarding how to craft black letter law, see Chapter 4.

Bloomberg: This is a law-based search engine.

***The Bluebook*®:** The standardized style book used by law students and attorneys to cite cases. As a general rule, practitioners tend to use the blue pages of the book, while the white pages are more detailed and are generally used for the detailed citations of law review and other scholarly articles.

Boolean: The primary search method when doing specialty research because it allows you to specify what is being searched by setting the search engine to only use specific phrases, words within a set proximity of each other, or topics not to be included in the results.

CALI: Center for Computer-Assisted Legal Instruction. CALI has lessons (some of which may even be assigned by professors), practice questions, and awards.

CALI Award: An award from the Center for Computer-Assisted Legal Instruction for the top student within a class. Students often refer to these awards as "getting a CALI" rather than saying "CALI Award." Only participating schools give CALI Awards.

California Baby Bar: The mini bar exam for 1Ls that plan to bar in California. This is a great resource for practice questions for doctrinal subjects.

Career Services: This is an office that is very helpful when planning your career post-graduation, as well as helping to connect you with practicing lawyers during your program. If needed, it is also a great stop for resume workshopping if you are switching careers.

Case Brief: The notes you take on each case you read during law school. Generally you will include the case name, cite, parties, procedural history, factual history, arguments, issue, holding, rule, reasoning, judgment, concurrence, and dissent. See Chapter 4.

Casebook: Law school textbook. Generally named this because traditionally they were mostly composed of cases. Newer textbooks have slightly more introductory and reference material.

Civil Procedure: A first year course focusing on the way the court works within the civil realm (i.e. torts, contracts, and other non-criminal cases). Even if this is not a course in your first semester, many of the other courses have a basis in civil procedure due to the focus on the court's procedure within the case (such as motions).

CLE: Continuing Legal Education. Sometimes also referred to as MCLE. Some states require attorneys to take classes that provide CLE credits. These are often found at conventions, conferences, or symposiums. Not every state requires CLE credits.

Clerkship: Working under the supervision of a judge or attorney, usually performing research and writing tasks. These are usually prestigious roles. See Chapter 10.

Clinic: A law school class, or sometimes an extracurricular, that gives students real-life experience by working with clients under the supervision of professors. Clinics can be in many areas, but some common ones include immigration or criminal defense/appeals.

Cold Call: Under the Socratic method, a cold call is when the professor will select a name at random and have a one on one conversation with the person. The conversation is a dialogue in which the professor is asking probing questions to make the students think. See Chapter 2.

Concurrence: The portion of the opinion where any judges in the majority may write their reasoning for agreeing with the primary opinion. A concurrence may include a different way of analyzing the facts or a different reasoning. There may be multiple concurrences, or none.

Constitutional Law: A first year law school course focusing on the United States Constitution. It is often split into two areas: how the government can operate within the Constitution (powers) and the rights of the people (liberties).

CRAC: Conclusion - Rule - Analysis - Conclusion format for essay writing. This style is more common for exam essay writing. Remember to find out your professor's preference and tailor your writing to their preference. See Chapter 7.

CRAP: Conclusion - Rule - Analysis - Policy format for essay writing. This style is more common for exam essay writing, but is highly professor specific. Not every professor wants the history or policy behind a rule given, whereas others strongly suggest you add those arguments at the end if, and only if, you have time. Never add a policy explanation before answering all the required parts of the question or you will lose points. Remember to find out your professor's preference and tailor your writing to their preference. See Chapter 7.

CREAC: Conclusion - Rule - Explanation - Analysis - Conclusion essay writing format. This format is more common for your legal writing class when doing memos or briefs. See Chapter 7.

CREXAC: Conclusion - Rule - Explanation - Example - Analysis - Conclusion essay writing format. This format is more common for your legal writing class when doing memos or briefs. See Chapter 7.

Criminal Law: A first year law school course covering crimes and what is generally required for certain types of crime. Crimes like burglary, robbery, larceny, murder, manslaughter, and rape are all possible topics in this class.

Dean's Fellow: A student that has taken on the yoke of leadership to help new law students adjust to law school. They will generally lead office hours for a small group of students in order to help go over study tips, or offer guidance relating to courses. These students are generally willing to have you reach out for anything you may need, including questions or encouragement when you have a bad day and are questioning your decision to go to law school. Remember, they are students like you and are not involved in developing school policy.

Defendant: The party against whom a case is brought. The term is used in both civil and criminal cases.

Dicta: Portion of a decision that is not precedent. Dicta is generally seen when judges discuss conclusions that are not necessary to the issue being discussed. Occasionally these may be hypotheticals that state if something else had happened then a different result would have occurred for whatever reason.

Dissent: The portion of an opinion where any judges who voted against the decision can include their argument of why they disagree with the majority. It is generally a persuasive argument on their side, but it is not binding and therefore not a precedent. There can be multiple dissents, depending on how many judges disagreed with the majority, or none.

Doctrinal: The core courses that make up almost all of law school, and often a large portion of the bar exam. These classes are generally civil procedure, constitutional law, contracts, criminal law, real property, and torts.

Elements: All the parts of a rule. Each element must be met for the rule to apply.

Externship: This is similar to an internship with required academic pieces. Check with your program early to determine if you are required to complete an externship, and if so, what specific criteria may need to be met in order to qualify.

Factors: Parts of a rule that are balanced to determine the liability of a person for the particular rule/crime/offense. Not every factor must be met, and some factors may be more important than others.

Factual History: The portion of a case brief that includes the facts that led to a lawsuit. This only needs to be key background facts and anything that is legally dispositive or could change the outcome of the case.

Fastcase: A law-based search engine/research site.

FRCP: Federal Rules of Civil Procedure. These rules are the basis for your civil procedure class and give direction regarding how civil cases move through the federal court system.

Holding: The court's decision within a case.

Honor Code: This is the academic standard you promise your work has attained throughout your time in law school. This can include the originality of your work, that you maintained quiet during the appropriate period, and more. Be sure to review your honor code upon admission so you are not caught by surprise.

Internship: An internship is an agreed upon experience between you, the law student, and someone who practices law. These can be as formal or informal as you jointly decide, as well as paid or unpaid. Do note, however, that they are different from externships. Internships, especially in your last year, have the potential to lead to job offers, and therefore should be taken seriously.

IP: Intellectual Property. An upper-level course focusing on the area of law covering trademarks, copyrights, and patents.

IRAC: Issue - Rule - Analysis - Conclusion format for essay writing. This style is more common for exam essay writing. Remember to find out your professor's preference and tailor your writing to their preference. See Chapter 7.

Judgment: This is the final holding of a court.

Judgment as a Matter of Law: Sometimes abbreviated as JMOL. This is a judgment during the trial, in which the judge determines that a party has failed to present facts that would allow the party to win the case.

K: The abbreviation for contract.

Kaplan: A test prep company used by many law students for MPRE and bar prep.

Law Review: A program involving the writing, editing, and citation checking of scholarly articles covering different areas of law. Schools may invite students onto law review based upon GPA, or there may be a writing competition to get onto law review. Some employers or internships may give preference to students who have participated in law review. See Chapter 11.

Lexis: This is a law-based search engine.

Litigation: A practice area in law that focuses on taking cases into the courtroom.

LLM: A Master of Laws degree is often referred to as an LLM. An LLM degree is an advanced law degree. Think of it as an advanced concentration program that you may be adding to your JD. You can focus on a variety of practice areas in order to gain more expertise.

LSAC: Law School Admission Council. This is the organization you go through to apply to law school. Once you have started school, this organization generally will not impact your law school career much unless you decide to transfer schools. Note that if you are considering transferring, many schools only allow you to transfer credits equivalent to your 1L year.

M&A: Mergers and Acquisitions. An upper-level class, but you may run across this abbreviation.

Malpractice: This is activity or inactivity by a lawyer that is adverse to the profession or client. It is a spectrum that ranges from negligence to improper conduct to illegal action. Punishment for malpractice can range from a reprimand to disbarment depending on severity.

Majority: In an appellate court decision, the majority is the winning side. Appellate courts generally have multiple judges, and therefore require that over half the justices support the opinion.

MBE: This is the Multistate Bar Exam and is currently used in all 50 states, although not in Puerto Rico. It focuses on fundamental doctrinal principles of law in multiple choice format.

MCLE: Minimum Continuing Legal Education. This is also referred to as CLEs. Some states require attorneys to take classes that provide CLE credits. These are often found at conventions, conferences, or symposiums. Not every state requires CLE credits.

MEE: This is the Multistate Essay Exam. It is used by a majority of the states and focuses on effective communication through written form.

Mind Map: This is a visual rendition of an outline that is similarly shaped to a spider web. You can see samples of one in Chapter 4.

Minority: In an appellate court decision, the minority is the losing side. The minority may write a dissent to the opinion, but is not required to.

Moot Court: A program in which students compete in a simulated court experience, often including both brief writing and oral arguments. Some employers or internships may give preference to students who have participated in moot court.

MPC: Model Penal Code. The MPC will be a basis for your criminal law class as many states have used the MPC to help shape their criminal law statutes.

MPRE: Multistate Professional Responsibility Exam. The ethics exam required by almost all states. Scores range from a low of 50 up to a high of 150. Exam scores can become outdated, depending on the state, so check that your score will still be valid when you plan to take the bar. NCBE is in charge of the exam and scores. The minimum passing score varies by state, but ranges between 75 and 86. The exam is composed of 60 multiple choice questions, of which 50 are scored and 10 are unscored.

MPT: This is the Multistate Performance Test that is utilized in a majority of states based on fundamental skills in lawyering.

NCBE: National Conference of Bar Examiners. This organization oversees the UBE, MBE, MEE, MPT, and MPRE exams.

NextGen Bar: This is the new bar that is intended to replace the UBE. The goal of this exam is to more heavily test practical skills. Currently there is little information about how the exam will be formatted beyond evaluating skills in a holistic manner.

OCI: On Campus Interview. An event at the law school in which employers set up and perform interviews onsite. Interviews could be for a post law school job or an internship.

Opinion: A court decision. This is where a court will record what they decided and why. Court opinions are used when writing memos, as well as what you read in casebooks to learn the black letter law.

OSCAR: Online System for Clerkship Application and Review. This is the system to apply for federal clerkships. The application period opens in June the year prior to your graduation. The current website address is: oscar.uscourts.gov

Outline: This is the general note-taking document that helps you to see the overarching themes of a course. They normally are not provided for classes, but you can either make them yourself, get a copy from another student, or purchase a commercial one online. Be sure it is not against the honor code to use someone else's outline prior to doing so.

Plaintiff: The party filing a case against a defendant in civil court.

Plurality: The opinion with the most justice support, but not enough support to make it the majority of the court. A plurality opinion is generally non-binding in terms of precedent.

Precedent: The law from a case that can be used to help decide future cases with similar facts so that results between cases are fairly predictable and consistent. When researching and writing briefs, precedent will support your argument in the case.

Pro Bono: This is work that a person does free of charge for another person or entity. There may be specific rules at your institution for counting pro bono work toward a program. Generally, it includes all work, but often is limited in law schools to law-based work.

Pro Se: This is when a person represents themself in court without a lawyer.

Procedural History: The portion of a case brief that includes what happens in the legal process to get to the case being discussed. This may include who files, key motions, and what each lower court held.

Prosecutor: An attorney representing the government in a criminal case against an accused defendant. Some locations may refer to the prosecutor as a "state's attorney." When it comes time for an internship, a prosecutor's office may be a great option, especially if you are interested in criminal law.

Quiet Period: This is the time between an exam or assignment going "live" (being available) and when you either receive your scores back or all exams have been collected. This will be communicated to you by your university. During this time, no one is able to communicate with other classmates, faculty, or anyone else regarding that assignment. Some universities may have different end times between classmates versus faculty, so be aware of which type of quiet period has ended.

Quimbee: A student resource for practice questions and abbreviated case summaries for select cases. These should not be used in place of reading assigned cases.

Real Property: A first year law school course focusing on how property ownership and possession transfer between parties.

Reasoning: This is where a court explains why they ruled in the manner they did.

Remand: When an appellate court sends a case back to the lower court. This may be required to finalize a decision, or can mean that the lower court needs to do additional steps to make a decision on the case.

Remedies: The types of relief a party may receive. This includes monetary damages or injunctions.

Restatement: A series of treatises covering different areas of laws (including torts, contracts, and professional responsibility) and how the law should be interpreted. There are different editions of the restatement, and some classes may discuss multiple editions of the restatement throughout the semester.

Rule: This is either an explicit or implicit statement of law that can be pulled from a case to be applied in other cases. Be sure not to confuse it with dicta.

SBA: Student Bar Association. A student organization, similar to a student government or student council. Generally every class within the program has representation and there is an executive board.

Socratic Method: The Socratic method is when the teacher and student have a dialogue in which the teacher asks a series of probing questions to the same student(s) to get to the point of the case at hand. It is the most common question method in law school. See Chapter 2.

Statutory Interpretation: Methods of reading and understanding a statute. This will include a variety of methods such as using canons of construction, interpretation guides, and legislative history. Generally on undecided laws, different methods of statutory interpretation can result in different results.

Summary Judgment: A motion prior to the trial in which the court rules for a side based on a lack of a genuine dispute of facts. The full rule can be seen in FRCP Rule 56.

Supplements: These are external materials outside of your textbook that help to build upon the material assigned for classes.

Synch: Course material done in a synchronous or live manner, in which all students are engaged and participating simultaneously. Not every course will have a synch component.

T14: This term refers to the top 14 ranked law schools. If Ivy League comes to mind, you are on the right track. There can be changes to the rankings, so if you are curious a quick internet search should let you know who's currently dominating the list.

Teaching Assistant: An upper-level student who works with a professor. Their roles vary by class.

Template: A document used to prepare the rules you have learned from a semester in order to make essay writing easier. It will often be a compilation of the rule statements for the course.

Themis: A study resource that gives access to practice materials. It is especially well known for its MPRE and bar prep resources. This resource also has some helpful 1L study material.

Torts: A first year course that focuses on actions causing injury against another person. Torts include intentional actions, negligence, and strict liability cases that lead to litigation between the parties.

Transactional: The area of law that focuses on transactions, and avoiding the courtroom. Included in this area are business organization, contract writing, and estate planning. This area of law heavily focuses on document preparation and making deals between your client and other parties.

UBE: Uniform Bar Exam. The current bar exam format which allows the exam taker to take their scores and use it to certify in multiple states without rebarring. Many, but not all, states use the UBE, while others may use only part of it. It comprises the MBE, MEE, and MPT. These exam components are the current model for professors when creating exams, especially the MBE and MEE.

Under-Does-When: The format used when writing an issue statement, whether it is in a brief or on a case brief. This format indicates the type of law, a situation, and the legally dispositive facts.

U.S. Circuit Court of Appeals: The intermediate level of court within the federal system. It takes appeals from the U.S. District Court.

U.S. District Court: The lowest level of courts within the federal system. There is at least one district court per state.

U.S. Supreme Court: The highest court in the federal court system. The Supreme Court is made up of nine justices. The Supreme Court does not have to hear all appeals, but is able to hear appeals from both the federal system as well as state courts. As long as the state case issue is based on federal law.

Vacate: When an appellate court overturns or reverses a decision.

WestLaw: This is a law-based search engine.

Writing Sample: A document with sample pieces of legal writing that you may need when applying for internships or jobs. For most applications you will only want to include one type of writing (e.g., a piece from a draft contract or a brief to the court), but having multiples prepped can be very helpful if you are applying to different types of firms. It is also better to have a longer piece that can quickly be edited down, or have several documents of different lengths ready, in order to fit the requirements of the employer. Pay careful attention to the length requested by the employer to avoid providing a document that is either too long or too short.

▷▷▷ 2

The Ins and Outs of Online

For some of you, you may come from a background in technology and this section will be a breeze. For others of you, this is your first time delving into anything outside of Zoom. No matter which side you are coming from, this chapter is likely to be a bit outdated due to how quickly technology continues to develop no matter how recently we wrote it.

2.1 Instructional Formats

We are starting with the basics, and that means starting with instructional delivery. Every program is a little different, so we are giving a high-level overview of the most common modalities. Whatever the instructional format(s), always read your syllabus. Read the whole thing, even if it is 20+ pages long. We also recommend printing copies of your syllabus. Syllabi lay out the content for the course and what you need to accomplish during the semester. Each professor is a little different and the syllabus is the foundation of their expectations.

2.1.1 Asynchronous Learning

Asynchronous learning is often referred to as "asynch" and this is the content that is available to you on demand. There are recorded lectures and other content such as practice questions, short answers, and even video responses to be completed. Some courses only cover content in asynch format and others have a blended approach incorporating multiple modalities.

Asynch is like a gold mine; we love it and we think you will too. Unlike a lecture, you can pause the lecture video at any time and go look up any information that you are not clear about. There is generally closed captioning available, which is great for making sure you are clearly understanding the content being shared. In a live lecture, if you were not quite sure which word a professor spoke there is no pause button to back up and re-listen to the content. Take advantage of this unique feature because it is a huge boost.

You will want to take notes during your asynch instructional time. Often there are slide decks available to accompany the lecture. It can be great to take notes right along with the lecture slides. Also, it is helpful to have your outline open while you are working through asynch because you can copy and paste straight from the lesson into your outline. (If you do not know what outlining is quite yet, hang in there—it is covered in Chapter 4.) Make a note of any content that you do not understand and ask your professor for clarification.

It is also a good idea to go back and review the responses from your peers, particularly if there is a segment that you are unsure about. Seeing how others have formulated responses and possible counterarguments that you may have overlooked gives you a huge opportunity to boost your learning. It is also a great way to confirm that you are grasping the material on par with your peers. This is a unique feature of transparency that is not as readily available in a traditional classroom format.

SARAH'S TIP — x

If you are pressed for time, you can try increasing the speed on the lecture videos. I usually watch lecture videos at 1.75 speed. Just don't be surprised when you get to class and your professor lectures at a normal rate of conversation! It's a huge time saver on the asynch, particularly if you like to watch videos multiple times.

2.1.2 Synchronous Learning

Synchronous learning is conducted in real-time and can be through live classes or video conferencing such as a Zoom meeting. In either forum, remember this is a professional setting. You may be subject to a dress code, but even if you are not subject to a dress code you probably want to make a point of dressing somewhat professionally. A suit is probably overkill, but avoiding shirts with obscene imagery and profanity may help you cultivate a professional identity as you prepare for practice.

Try to limit your distractions during lectures. Cell phones can be a huge distraction if you are scrolling through social media. On the other hand, engaging in peer discussion can be a huge benefit. If it is not prohibited in your program, you can message in a peer group and seek clarification on lecture points as the discussion is progressing. If everyone in your group is confused, that is a cue to raise your hand and ask. Obviously, this should not be abused or used to distract your peers but it can be a great method to confirm learning in real time. If your study group uses this method and it is too distracting for you, simply let them know and turn your device's setting off during lectures.

Always go to class. Many programs do not have excused absences and after missing a certain number of minutes, your grade is impacted. If you have a major life emergency, your professors may appreciate a courtesy notification. Ask your professors for their preferences if it is not clearly in the syllabus.

2.1.3 Video Conferencing

As you are taking notes, it can be tempting to try and write down everything the professor says. Some students actually retain the knowledge better by noting a few key words. The best part of attending class via video conferencing is the lectures are generally recorded. Similar to asynch, this allows you to go back and re-listen to parts of the lecture or even the entire thing. You might find it is a great way to fall asleep at night...

You will want to sign into the video conference 5–10 minutes before class starts to make sure you do not have any log-in issues. You should generally expect to be ready to turn your camera on once class starts. Some professors stay online after the lecture time ends to answer questions. We highly recommend listening to the questions from your classmates because they may be asking questions you did not even realize you had! As a point of etiquette, it is helpful to leave your camera on if you have a question and turn your camera off if you do not have any questions. It helps the professor gauge how many students have questions, because unlike a physical classroom you will not be standing in line at the lecture podium. Remember, some professors will not record after-class questions so the only way to get the answers is to be there or get notes from a classmate regarding what was asked.

Snacks and dinner. We get it. You are busy, and this may be the first chance you have had to eat in hours. Obviously, best practice is try to find a window of time to eat before class starts or try to eat during a class break if you are lucky enough to get one. If that does not pan out and it is not prohibited by your program to eat during class, try to angle your camera so that everyone does not have a front row view of you chomping down on your jumbo burrito.

2.1.4 In-Person Classes

This is the "uphill in the snow both ways" old school style of learning. In-person classes allow for elbow to elbow interaction with your peers, and generally professors take questions at the podium after class. Take advantage of these opportunities to build deeper personal connections. There is not generally a recording to go back and listen to and there is no closed captioning. It requires the same level of attention as the previous modalities, but you need a back-up plan for class notes if you happen to miss a class for some emergent reason.

You will want to arrive ahead of class and get all of your materials ready. The front row seats tend to be where the "A" students sit, but do not feel constrained that a seating chart will determine your grade. Sit where you are most comfortable—the key to success is your engagement with the material.

2.2 Socratic Method

The Socratic method is commonly used in both classes held in person and online via video conferencing. Traditionally the Socratic method involves a professor cold calling on students. Socratic method is when the teacher and student have a dialogue, in which the teacher asks a series of probing questions to the same student. Under the Socratic method, a cold call is when the professor will select a name at random and have a one on one conversation with the person. In a traditional classroom setting this could last for half the class.

In an online format, the professors are much more willing to have shorter dialogues with students that only last a few minutes. Generally professors who are doing the shorter method will stick with the same student either for one related topic, or until the student has worded the answer in the way the professor is looking for. This allows for situations where the professor may actually call on every student in the class once, and even some students multiple times. What does this mean for you? An increased need to stay engaged.

To be ready for your cold call, make sure you test your microphone and audio prior to the start of class. When you are being cold called on, keep listening until you know the professor has called on a new student, because those questions are still for you. Just because a professor is continuing to question you does not mean you are wrong. Sometimes the professor is just checking that you are confident in your answer and reinforcing an important point. It may be embarrassing, but no one will ever remember it except you. Be ready to unmute your mic. If you are unsure what the professor is asking, you are encouraged to ask them to repeat or reword the question. Sometimes the way a professor words things is hard to understand, and they have to reword it before you get a chance to ask because they realize it was awkward and unhelpful in that format.

As the Socratic method has loosened, so have teachers' desire to call on students at random. They may start at a random point within the class roster, but will ultimately go alphabetically or reverse alphabetically. You can watch for and learn the professors' preferences by knowing who is before and after you alphabetically to see if you are always called on in close succession. Some teachers may even assign specific slides, questions, or days that they will call on specific students.

BETHANY'S TIP — x

Professors love alphabetical order. If your first or last name is near the beginning or end of the alphabet, be prepared to be cold called on the first day... of every class. Prior to changing my last name, I was in the middle of the alphabet and sometimes I wish I hadn't changed it just for that purpose.

JESSICA'S TIP — x

If a professor will allow you to volunteer an answer, do it. Choose the problem that you are most comfortable with answering and explaining. This allows you to participate appropriately, while reducing your stress level. Additionally, when you volunteer information the professor is less likely to cold call on you.

On a video conferencing screen, everyone's picture and name are easily visible for the professor to see. Since this is the case, professors may allow for volunteers before cold calling a student. This allows you to choose when you want to answer so that you are answering the questions you are most comfortable with. For people who get nervous speaking in front of others this can be helpful.

SARAH'S TIP — X

Get comfortable with a little bit of silence. The awkward pause after a professor poses a question is uncomfortable for me. Instead of constantly volunteering answers, I count to ten in my head because this gives my peers an opportunity to jump in. I also tally my responses throughout the class and once I hit three, I stop volunteering answers.

To get the most out of the Socratic method, you need to stay continuously engaged with the conversation. When you are not the person answering the questions, this can be a challenge. Besides taking notes, it helps to answer the questions yourself and compare your answer to the other student's answer. Also, try to figure out what the line of reasoning is behind the professor's questions. Sometimes it is just gathering the procedural or factual history of a case, but sometimes it is refining the specifics of a rule and its exceptions. The professor has an end goal in mind when asking the questions of what they want you to learn and understand from a particular case.

JESSICA'S STORY — X

Every professor does it differently. The first, and only, professor I had who actually did traditional cold calls with the online students had me as the first cold call. I was in the middle of the roster and unprepared for the nonstop questions lasting 30 minutes. That was nerve wracking! I had another professor who called on me EVERY single class.

2.3 Learning Management Systems

It is likely that your program will be using some kind of learning management system to house your materials. Common systems include Canvas, Blackboard, 2U, and many more. Even during our time in the program, we used a conglomeration of three different systems. It is extremely important that you get in early and click around throughout the system to learn how it functions. If nothing else, locate their "help" section so if you have any issues with the site, you know how to contact them. (Note: Any content questions should be through your instructor and not the LMS.)

You should receive a log-in from your institution that will help you gain access to a variety of resources throughout the system. Not only will there be courses/materials, but many institutions also offer additional resources such as access to student organizations, the law library, or academic offices through it. Be sure to ask during your orientation what other resources you can access through your LMS.

BETHANY'S STORY — x

If you are having issues within the LMS, reach out ASAP to the professor. The professors may not know there is an issue and don't have (or know how to access) the student view. Professors may not be trained in the LMS, so it might be as much of a learning curve for you as it is for them.

2.3.1 Institutional Technology

Your law school may have other institutional platforms as well. It can be a little overwhelming in the beginning when you are getting set up with log-ins for a million (well, probably not quite a million) different places to access various things. You might find it helpful to create a document that contains each of the sites with a quick summary of the type of resource.

2.3.2 Google Docs Web-Based Word-Processing Program & Google Drive Online Storage Service

Many institutions already partner with Google LLC for their range of resources. If this is you: perfect, you are off to a great start. If not, go make a free email with Google LLC's Gmail email service. Right now. (No, this is not a paid sponsorship. All Google LLC services mentioned here are trademarks of Google LLC and this book is not endorsed by or affiliated with Google LLC in any way. We just feel really strongly about how it can positively impact your success!)

Starting your first semester, create either a drive or folder that will exclusively be your law materials. From there, create a folder for each class each semester and keep it organized. Add materials you receive from each class, your individual and joint outlines, and even your assignments.

Start creating a document that serves as your outline starting week one of classes. Choose to share it or keep it secret—either way, create it directly in your folder for that class. If someone shares an outline with you, click the option to save a shortcut to your folder. This will not move the file for the person who created it, but it will move it from your "shared" folder to your organization method. If you are sharing an editable document with others, be sure you either know how to use the restore feature to reverse changes to a certain point, or keep a secondary copy for yourself. This way, if things do not go the way you were hoping for whatever reason, you always have something to go back to in the future.

Editable documents are also great for group projects. You can see exactly what others are changing or if they even logged in, and you can leave comments and/or assign areas to different colleagues.

Just be careful as editable documents do not download identically to a Word document. If you have programmatic requirements to submit in Word format, be sure to download early and ensure it still meets the layout requirements. If you have the option of submitting in PDF format, that is the best conversion.

SARAH'S STORY — x

I used to use the hunt method of searching through my recent docs to find resources shared by classmates. Bethany very kindly taught me about the "Shared with me" process to streamline my search. Thanks Bethany, still using that tip every week!

2.4 Building Relationships at a Distance

By this point in your life, building relationships may be second nature. Unfortunately, the skills you already have might need to be modified a bit to foster online relationships. There is a need to be more conscientious with establishing the relationships than you might normally be in a residential setting. We are including each of our personal experiences and tips in this area since we all approached it in a slightly different way.

2.4.1 Time Zones

One of the perks of being online is the ability to attend from anywhere. Part of this benefit, however, also includes the dreaded time zone conversion. Keep in mind that most schools will function based on the time zone of their physical location and may not always put the time zone in their communications. When in doubt, be sure to reach out to confirm rather than assume! To be kinder to your colleagues, and yourself, be sure to always include a time zone when proposing study group times or referencing other meeting requirements. Luckily, Google Calendar will convert the times for you to the home time zone you have it set for. Another trick of the trade is to get an extension on your computer to show not only your current time zone, but also others that you can quickly look up.

BETHANY'S TIP — x

I have a few time zones saved to my computer's task bar. This way, I can quickly convert to my study group members' time zones to ensure that when I propose a time to meet it isn't too early or conflicting with a traditional workday.

2.5 Suggestions from the Authors

Jessica's Suggestions

Personally, I tend to be more reserved, at least until I get to know someone. Reaching out is way outside of my comfort zone. Oddly enough, I actually started my law school career by reaching out of my comfort zone. When looking back at some of the notes I took during law school orientation, the first thing I wrote down was "Sarah from SD and an email address," which I immediately followed up with an email that day to find out more about that little commonality. "Sarah from SD" is Sarah Covington, one of the co-authors of this book, but also one of the first people I reach out to with my triumphs and failures.

I strongly recommend using orientation and that first week to make notes on your classmates' backgrounds when doing group ice breakers. Who lives near you? Who has a similar job? A common interest? A shared experience? A similar goal? School email addresses are formulaic and easy to guess, or they may even auto fill if you type the person's name. Take a few minutes to write an email and point out that common link. Start the conversation. Even if you do not become close friends, you will not regret having some background with the person when you get randomly assigned for a group project.

When orientation starts, inevitably someone in the group starts a group chat (and if no one has, you do it). The platform does not matter. Join it, and interact. You will get to learn more about your classmates, and it will be on each person's terms, not the face that is being presented to professors and deans. The group chat is a great resource to ask questions amongst yourselves, learn about each other, and eventually converse, commiserate, and joke. Write a bio or send a picture of yourself that shows an important, non-law school aspect of your life, and invite one or two others to do the same until everyone has done it.

A unique plus of online law school is the broad network that you have. It can be challenging that you do not have a built-in local network, but if you know you may move (think: military families), you potentially have contacts in other geographic areas within the legal field. You can also use this network when you have a client who knows someone, and you need to do a referral.

Bethany's Suggestions

My husband and I knew that the lack of connection was going to be the hardest piece of online school for me. In residential law school, you get to talk before class in the hallways, grab a coffee, or talk through concepts post-class. Online, you are in waiting rooms prior to class, timing is trickier to catch a meeting due to working schedules, and it is nearly bedtime post-class. The joke growing up was that I had never met a stranger, which stems from academia always being my social playground. I started the online program with a sense of disconnection and quickly made it my goal to fix that issue. Here are a few tips that worked for me as a social butterfly:

Know your strengths and use them to build connections. I have a strong background in technology and online instruction. I used this to volunteer to serve as a group administrator for group projects, sending calendar invites, starting Google Docs, and integrating different technologies into presentations. This helped with creating space for classmates to connect easily when that was not their strength. Then, when I struggled with small talk—because let's be real, I do not like that almost as much as I do not like multiple choice questions—someone else who was strong in that area could take the lead. Take a moment to think about your strengths and how you can use these to your advantage.

Connection is a huge piece, but meaningful connection means the most. This means finding a way to meet each person in the cohort and find the folks who work similarly. This does not mean think identically to you! The bottom line is not everyone is in law school to network and help one another—this was hard to learn. Although I was not the first person to reach out to each person in our cohort, I did take every opportunity to chat with them in GroupMe and on the chat in our online Zoom classes and to connect on social media. Set a goal of what you want to achieve here: form a study group, collaborate on an outline, network your way into a job, etc. Then do it!

You will find your people—or your people will find you. That first semester can feel like a crapshoot, but the more you put yourself out there, or at least keep yourself open to the opportunities presented to you, the faster this will happen.

Sarah's Suggestions

Law school is unlike other educational experiences, even other graduate programs. You will need relationships with your classmates because they will understand the unique experience that you are going through. Even more so, the shared experience will help build your relationships. Study groups are important, and we will get into that topic more later on, but even more so, you will need to cultivate connections with people. It is important to start building connections early.

When you are not elbow to elbow, relationship building requires a little more intentionality. You will probably hear the term "networking" quite often, and that is because it is important. Here are some practical steps to getting started with building relationships with your classmates from a distance.

Start by sending a message or email to another student. The field of law is a big, beautiful world. Consider reaching out to students that have expressed interest in other practice areas to learn a little more about that specific area of law. They may have some insights on practice areas you have never even considered and may end up loving! It is always fun to connect with people and learn what they are passionate about.

Additionally, consider developing connections with those in close geographic proximity to you. These are the individuals that you will likely be practicing with after graduation. Students in traditional programs tend to end up with a vast in-state network, whereas there may only be a handful of students in your state. If you are fortunate enough to have a classmate nearby, try to schedule dinner or in-person study groups every once in a while.

Schedule time to get to know one another. It can feel like your schedule is already bursting at the seams and like you cannot add one more thing. These sessions can be a brief ten minute connection right before class. I love scheduling right before class because it provides a natural hard stop. You are able to spend a couple of minutes in human connection prior to class without the social aspect taking over your limited time.

My personal style is to develop deep connections with a small group of people. Other students have developed much broader networks. Remember, it is OK to approach your relationship building in the method that works best for you.

Key Takeaways

- Do your best on cold calls, and have a little grace with yourself. It is a new learning style!
- Make a point to build connections with your peers because you are all in this together.
- Press into tech to help you flourish.

▷▷▷ 3

Curious About Context?

With all the new commitments you have taken on, we suspect you are wondering, "Will this book *really* help me?" and "Who are these authors to say they can *actually* help?" We are you ... in a few years. All of us are current online law students, in the midst of a career shift, balancing work, family, basic living necessities and school. And we want to provide you with everything, or at least mostly everything, that we wished we knew or had access to when we started our online law journey.

Notably, we have intentionally chosen a colloquial style of writing because we remember being brain-fried with all the new legal terms we encountered in case we were reading our first semester. We recommend tackling the heavy reading on your to-do list first and then taking on less arduous tasks as your mental energy wanes.

You may also notice the book is front-loaded, meaning the chapters at the beginning of the book are much longer than in the latter half. That is intentional too. We want to help you acclimate as quickly as possible and help preserve your time in the latter half for mastering applying your doctrinal learning.

If you are interested, this chapter tells you a bit more about the authors. For some of you, context matters. Knowing what lenses this book was written from is important. For others of you, you were assigned this book to read and it might be the last thing on your checklist to get to before you complete your homework for the week. No worries—it does not hurt our feelings if you skip the next few pages.

Jessica Carmichael, BS

Originally from Massachusetts, my husband and I moved to western South Dakota after we got married. Until online law school became available, there was no possible way I could do law school since my nearest law school is over six hours away, and uprooting my life was not an option.

Most of my career has been entrepreneurial. I owned a business from the time I graduated undergrad until my husband and I decided to have children. In addition to being a business owner, I was elected to city council and did a variety of volunteer work (some of which I still do). I have two young children: a son who was three years old when I started law school, and a daughter who was one year old. I am a first generation law student, but I do have in-laws who are attorneys.

Since starting law school in the University of Dayton's Hybrid Program, I have won two CALI awards for the top grades in Torts and Real Property, held the Hybrid Program's SBA Treasurer position, and been a Dean's Fellow mentoring incoming 1Ls within the Hybrid Program for two years. I am currently a 2L who has been able to accelerate a semester, so my anticipated graduation date is December 2023.

Identities Shaping My View: First generation law student, wife, stay at home mother of two toddlers, financial aid recipient, rural resident, white, female, and business owner.

Learning Style: I have to have physical materials for studying. If it is digital (like my outline or course reading material), I print it. I make flashcards. I find practice study sessions helpful, but generally only do them near exams because of personal time constraints.

Favorite 1L Class: Real Property

Worst 1L Class: Criminal Law

Post Law School Goals: Transactional work, preferably part time or remotely. Volunteering with assorted boards/organizations.

Advice: Network early. Some classes may require you to interview attorneys and already having a rapport with at least one can help. Plus, having a network when you graduate will be incredibly beneficial.

Bethany Carr, BME | MS

Back in high school, I participated in both Mock Trial and Peer Court. I enjoyed my time, but I had my heart set on being an educator. Since then, and two education-based degrees later, I have come to the conclusion that the biggest impact on education does not always happen inside of the classroom.

Most of my professional career has been focused in Student Affairs in Higher Education. After speaking with my, now, lawyer husband about my favorite parts of what I do, the answer boiled down to impact on the field of education. As we know, education is not known for cutting-edge salaries, so finding a program that would allow me to continue my employment full-time was imperative. Fun fact: Many universities do not offer tuition remission for law programs, which made it even more important to find a program that offered lucrative scholarships.

Since starting the program at the University of Dayton School of Law, I have expanded my involvement both personally and professionally. I have served as a pro bono intern at local private practices, been acknowledged in a published annual supplement as a research assistant and writer, and actively engaged with academic clubs in leadership roles. I am a 2L who has been taking the traditional four-year path through the part-time program.

Identities Shaping My View: Full-time employee, spouse, white, female/cis-gender, first generation college student, LSAT fee-waiver recipient, neurodivergent thinker, scholarship recipient, and educational advocate.

Learning Style: I am a multi-modal learner who studies best through teaching others. Kooky mnemonic sayings, tapping different rhythms, and having story-based understandings help keep me on track. I still have a picture of Cardozo "the clown" from when I used a visual to help remember his ruling I didn't agree with ... and it still shows up on my briefs well past my first year.

Favorite 1L Class: Real Property—it is a giant logic puzzle!

Worst 1L Class: Professional Responsibility. Let's just say I would prefer to write in my own answers to multiple choice questions.

Post Law School Goals: Higher education general counsel, with a focus in disability, intellectual property, and education law.

Advice: Have confidence! Or tell yourself you do *until* you do. I am someone who doubts that I understand something until I know every single thing I possibly can about a topic. The reality is you do not need all of that—especially not on the test. If you have an interest in something, great! Dig deeper. You probably know more than you think you do, and if you are struggling—others probably are, too!

Sarah Covington, MBA | BA

I will give the condensed version because the last thing you want to do right now is to read a lengthy biography. I started my MBA at 19, total nerd move. Midway through, my daughter had heart surgery and I wanted to contribute to the industry that had saved her life so I added a healthcare management concentration. I realized those with industry experience in healthcare seemed to be getting so much more out of the program. I decided to wait 10 years to start a PhD...

During my healthcare career, I progressed to a VP of Revenue Cycle Role (i.e., bringing in the cash) and then shifted to the healthcare innovation segment and served as a Chief Operating Officer and founding member. I also serve as adjunct undergraduate faculty, teaching healthcare law courses online. From leading winning teams at multiple MIT pitch competitions to calls with NASA astronauts, it was a wildly rewarding experience.

I began researching PhD programs (remember that 10 year goal), but then stumbled upon ABA accredited online JD options. A JD seemed much more practical so I jumped right in, mid-pandemic, while running a company and homeschooling our daughters. I've since transitioned to legal internships and extracurriculars. I have earned multiple CALI awards, graded-on to law review, am on the mock trial team, and have represented the school in various ABA competitions.

Identities Shaping My View: First generation law student, second generation American, wife, mother of two incredible daughters (one of whom is neurodivergent), financial aid recipient, and rural resident.

Learning Style: I am a hardcore visual learner, so reading works well for me but audio lectures do not usually stick. I learn best by book briefing, making my own mini-outline, doing multiple choice questions, reading practice essays for template inspiration, and reading supplemental material. I participate in very few formal study group sessions throughout the semester because the weekly thing does not work for my life.

Favorite 1L Class: Real Property, bring on the Rule Against Perpetuities!

Worst 1L Class: Torts II, the struggle bus was real... also my daughter had knee surgery right before finals so class was not my top priority in that season of life.

Post Law School Goals: Umm, well, I do not know. I had a solid plan coming into law school, but throughout the educational journey I realized I enjoy many different areas of law.

Advice: Find your people. This journey can be tough at times and having a close group of friends as you encounter the tough days is key. I also kind of wish somebody had told me early on that I did not have to make mega outlines. I feel like I encountered that expectation so often, but the mini-outlines and templates are what actually work for my learning. I am a rule follower, so it was not until my dominant hand was in a cast for half a semester that I ditched the "supposed to do" approach to my studying and shifted to doing what actually worked best for me. Who knew having a clunky cast would end up so beneficial!

3.1 Letter to Spouses, Family Members, and Support Systems

Hand the book to your significant other, spouse, or other person who will be your support system during your online law program to read this next portion.

Dear Support System,

The person who was assigned to read this book is about to embark upon a journey that is difficult and unique. Unless you have personally experienced an online law program, there will be challenges they face that will be different than any you have ever experienced, even if you attended a residential law program or took graduate classes online.

There are horror stories about what law school can do to a person, physically, mentally and physically. However, we're not here to tell you how ... stressful ... it can be. Instead, we're here to give you some quick pointers on how best to support your person during an online law program based on what we, ourselves, have appreciated as folks who have been there.

Create a new normal. Law school in general takes up a lot of time. Not only are they in law school, but they're also doing it online, which brings even more challenges. Likely, they are still responsible for other people, jobs, tasks, in addition to the added-in classes, homework, and internships. Schedules and responsibilities will need to be discussed and changed. Be open to taking on a bit more so they can truly focus on schoolwork when they are scheduled for homework or class time. Just because they are in the room next to you doesn't mean they're available to take the call, answer the door, or do the laundry in the moment that it happens.

Give grace. Law school has emotional strain, and it is emphasized in the online format. There may be times they feel alone or ostracized due to the online-only contact. They may feel over-stimulated from sensory overload caused by the various methods needed to succeed online. Find ways to connect with your person that helps to decompress from the heightened emotional state in a healthy manner, and know that there are support systems available if you or your person are experiencing the need for them. Be sure to utilize the support provided by the school, and your local community as well, as needed.

Be OK not knowing. The unknown is a scary reality. The bottom line is that you won't understand everything they're going through. And don't forget that they literally cannot tell you everything they're going through due to the honor code and legal requirements. Be there for them in the ways that you can and laugh it off when they have to generalize something or leave out a piece of a story that you actually needed for anything they told you to make sense. Lucky for you, you're likely to get to join in on the studying for exams so get excited to learn those really exciting tort elements we know you were excited to commit to memory.

Create time. Your person may have been the one to plan your time together prior to their law school journey. Now, that may be an additional burden they just don't have brainspace to do the planning itself. Take the initiative to make time together, during the semester and extended breaks. Just because their capacity is different now, it doesn't mean they feel any less for you. Actually, it's probably quite the opposite!

And, thank you. Online law school can be just as stressful on our people as it is for those of us who have actually been through it. All of us authors agree that without the support of our people, we wouldn't be where we are today.

We encourage you to use the space below to make your commitments to each other on how you plan to support one another during this journey and revisit it along the way.

COMMITMENTS

____________________ ____________________

Student Support Person

3.2 Statement of Limitations

It is important to note that although our team of authors is diverse in many ways, it is also akin in others. We purposely have provided a section in our book to name our identities to provide context in how they play a role in our online law school journey. We recognize that the intersectionality of all of our identities, both consciously and unconsciously, have had an impact on our program experience and how this book has been written.

Also, please note that the content of this book is based on the authors' student work and not necessarily model answers. Model answers are subjective and at the discretion of individual professors.

3.3 Reflection

This might be a good time to pause and reflect on your own learning journey so far. Either in your head, or scribbled on some paper, take a moment to answer the following questions.

- What classes were your favorite and least favorite prior to coming to law school and why?
- Have you ever had to study before and, if so, what techniques worked best for you?
- What is your end goal for going to law school? *Seriously, post this up somewhere nearby where you are doing the work for the program. On the hard days, this will help pull you through!*

Remember, your law school journey is going to be daunting at times. Ultimately, it gives you a new perspective even on things you were sure you "knew." You may think your learning style is always solo, but be willing to experiment because you never know how other methods could actually benefit you. The same goes for any expectation you may have, such as needing accommodations and grades.

Section Two

First Semester

▷▷▷ 4

The Start of Successful Habits

4.1 How to Read/Brief a Case

Every casebook you read is filled with cases, and simply reading the cases will not be enough. You will need to brief the cases as well as taking notes on the material in order to fully understand what you are getting from the case, as well as being prepared for cold calls during class. During your 1L year, or at least your first semester, you may find yourself rereading cases, and taking a lot longer to read than you ever expected. Reading 5 pages of the casebook may take an hour, before briefing, and that is OK.

While reading, look up words or phrases you do not know. It is likely your professor will ask about those phrases and will have expected you to look for the legal definition. A single word can change the entire meaning of a case, so if you are in doubt, always check.

There are three primary ways to brief cases: 1) hand written; 2) typed; and 3) book briefing. Each has benefits. Book briefing can be a little faster during the reading process, but more challenging during cold calls. A written brief can take longer to do, but is easier during the cold calls. Being entirely digital is great, but you can lose your typed briefs if you do not have them on the cloud and your computer dies. Multiple screens can sometimes be a challenge during synchronous classes, and can lead to awkward pauses while you switch between screens.

JESSICA'S TIP — x

Flag every case in the book, whether you are book briefing or traditional briefing. It will help you find your cases quickly during class.

Every brief will have the same components. Although it may be possible to limit the material in any given brief, you should wait until you know what the professor is going to look for in any given class. The parts of the brief are: the parties, citation, procedural history, facts, arguments, issue, holding, rule, reasoning, judgment, and any concurrence or dissent.

Brief Parts

Parties	Citation
Procedural History	Facts
Arguments	Issue
Holding	Rule
Reasoning	Judgment
Any Concurrence or Dissent	

Parties: When writing down the parties, note who is the plaintiff (P or π) and the defendant (D or Δ). Although the plaintiff is traditionally on the left, Supreme Court cases and some older cases will change the order based on who is appealing. Sometimes you may even want to note which is the appellant/appellee, or any specifics about the parties (i.e. in family law you may want to note the husband/wife, or mother/father for the given case; in IP it may be the senior user of a mark).

Citation: You may never need the full case cite, but practicing using the caption and writing a citation can be great practice for your writing course. The citation can also help you distinguish which court decided the case and on which date. The date can help indicate if it is an overturned case used for historical purposes or if it is showing a long precedent for the specific rule. For some classes you will need to learn the rules by state/style/district, so it will help you quickly identify which rule you are looking at. If multiple cites are given at the start of the case, you likely do not need all of them; just use the primary cite.

Procedural Facts: At the very least this should include the courts the case has gone through and the holding of the court. Some professors will require that you include any relevant motions in this portion. Unusual or important motions will often be asked about by professors.

Facts: This should include all relevant and necessary background facts. You will be looking for the key facts that the case turns on.

Arguments: You will want to include both side's arguments in your brief. This can help distinguish the reasoning for the majority and minority, especially where there is a split in the law.

Issues: Try to make your issue state short and understandable. Many professors will suggest you use the Under-Does-When format. This format is the same as what is often used in legal writing and allows you to identify not only the issue, but the area of law you are looking at, and a key fact that may shift the result. If you are not sure what area of law, look at what chapter and subheading the case is located to craft your "Under" portion. It is best if you can craft the issue so that it has a yes or no answer.

Under-Does-When Examples

- Under battery, is intent met when the actor knows an act is occurring and influences the event's results?
- Under self defense, is defense of property legal when severe injury occurs?
- Under negligence, is liability overridden when the violation is ordinary care?
- Under proximate cause, will a risk factor test all for possible liability on an unforeseen event?
- Under a lease, who has the responsibility to ensure actual possession when there is a holdover tenant?

Holding: This should generally be a yes or no answer. If you cannot word it as a yes or no answer, try for a one sentence answer.

Rule: This should be a one sentence statement of what the court decided as a general rule. Sometimes it may be a little longer if the rule is listing out elements. The case may provide multiple rules, so each would be their own sentence.

Reasoning: Use the reasoning to explain the way the court applies the rule to the facts of the case. It can help you understand the distinction of when the rule applies to facts. At exam time, it helps to understand when the rule applies.

Judgment: Use this section to note what the court decided. It should include which party won, and what the result was.

Concurrence/Dissent: Do not ignore these "extras," because they are not useless information. Include a quick summary of the argument, how the party would have decided, and why. The concurrence and dissent will offer another way to consider an issue, or will help show a split of how courts handle an issue. You will want to have a separate section for each concurrence or dissent listed, as there may be multiple ones in a case. If there are multiples, it is often helpful to include the name of which justice wrote it, even when it is not a Supreme Court case.

When you are writing or typing briefs, it is best to keep them together in one document, notebook, or binder. This will help you at exam time because everything will be in order and easy to locate. You want to remember to keep your brief short. A brief that is longer than the case will not be helpful, even if it is in more understandable language. You should be able to read the brief quickly and easily.

Book briefs can be very helpful for some types of learners, but there are some challenges. If you over highlight, it can be hard to understand what is important. To speed up this process, it can help to write next to the highlighted section what area is being discussed. You want to know when you are looking if it is a rule, reasoning, or an argument quickly. If you do not want to write this, another way is to color code the highlighting. If you are doing this, keep the color coding consistent between all cases within the textbook, and if possible between classes. It can also be helpful to write that color code in the front of the textbook so you can quickly reference back in case you forget (or are looking back a few semesters later).

One method of writing case briefs by hand includes large blank areas on the left and bottom to take notes during class. No matter how you write your briefs, use them during class. Take notes directly on the briefs. It can help to highlight the key points that professors are emphasizing and take your class notes in a different color than you originally used when writing the brief. By using a separate color, it allows the notes to stand out, because you will not be writing notes that are not important during class.

Most casebooks have some notes about the law and cases around each case. These notes can help clarify the cases, or give some additional context. You will want to take notes on any important information you find in that. It can either be a separate document, or a short "NOTE" at the bottom or the edge of the case brief.

4.2 How to Research Online

Despite what you may have been told previously, Google is your best friend in law school. Google is a great place to start when it comes to legal research because there is a chance that your topic is similar to what has been covered before. It will lead you to case briefs, law articles, private lawyers posting their thoughts on topics, and more. But do not stop there. This is merely your heading to make sure you are on the right track.

Once you have a general heading, move into WestLaw, Fastcase, or Lexis+. Many programs will include the cost of these programs in their tuition/fees. They are not cheap, so our word of advice is to get your money's worth so that you are a master of both when you graduate. This can save your future firm money since you will not need as many searches to find what you are looking for since they cost by search. We cannot emphasize enough to go through all of the certifications as they are great training tools for the software.

Boolean searching can seem like a foreign language initially, but once you get the hang of it your research time will be significantly shortened. Actually boolean searching can be done both in the specialized law research software and in most general browsers. Take a moment to try it out. First, try just typing your first name and surname into the search bar (first name surname). Then, try your first name and surname into the search bar in quotation marks ("first name surname"). Did you get different results? The second search is a boolean search that lets the search engine know those two words belong together. We encourage you to print out a free cheat sheet of these shortcuts to keep nearby throughout your program.

JESSICA'S PREFERENCE — x

I use both. I generally base it on whatever the professor's preference is because they are likely to want you to use a secondary source that is specific to their search engine of choice.

BETHANY'S PREFERENCE — x

I have loved Lexis since day one. For me, it feels more user-friendly and less cluttered. However, I did all of the certifications through WestLaw and Lexis as soon as I could and they helped bolster my resume during the first year.

SARAH'S PREFERENCE — x

I did certifications through both Lexis and WestLaw. I tend to use Google Scholar to search for cases more often than Lexis or WestLaw. While our searches are free as law students (thank you law school for providing this!), they won't be in practice. I've trained myself to start with Google Scholar to help develop a pattern of mitigating future expenses for clients. Once I've found a couple of cases heading in the right direction, I head to WestLaw with a targeted search to make sure I am not missing any relevant cases (because malpractice isn't on my bucket list).

4.3 Black Letter Law

Black letter law is a doctrinal rule that is generally established. Black letter law is the body of common law rules and it helps to think of these as basic rules that came over on the *Mayflower* from England so to speak. This might feel overwhelming to wrap your mind around, especially after outlining, so hang in there through this chapter. It helps to think of black letter law as the main rules and the cases you read help you understand the nuances of how those rules are applied.

Here is a simplified example from Torts of the interplay between black letter law and cases:

> **Black Letter Law:** An element of battery is contact. If there is no contact, there is no battery.
>
> **Case:** In *Garratt* the court finds moving the chair sufficient contact to constitute battery.[1] (It is OK if you have not covered this case yet or have only started reading it.)

The case helps us understand more about contact with respect to battery. Let us try one more simplified example:

> **Black Letter Law:** Property rights in wild animals are established by occupancy.
>
> **Case:** In *Pierson* the court finds mere pursuit insufficient to establish occupancy.[2]

Next, you will want to understand the role of the Restatements. There are many Restatements for the various areas of law and even different versions of Restatements. For example, there is a Restatement (Third) of Torts, which logically follows as the revised version of the Restatement (Second) of Torts. An important note is the Restatements themselves are not law. These are drafted by legal scholars and updated from time to time. The comments of the Restatement are informative because they provide examples as to how the law should be applied.

States can choose to, and often do, enact legislation that mirrors a version of the Restatement. Some states still follow the Restatement (Second) and other states have adopted the Restatement (Third), resulting in a jurisdictional split. These splits often have a majority (meaning there are more states that follow this approach) and a minority (meaning there are less states that follow this approach). These splits can happen even if the law is not adopted from a Restatement, but this is a common source of jurisdictional splits that you will encounter in your first semester in law school. Additionally, some

1. *Garratt v. Dailey*, 279 P.2d 1091 (Wash. 1955).
2. *Pierson v. Post*, 3 Cai. R. 175 (N.Y. Ct. App. 1805).

states may choose to make modifications to the Restatement rather than enacting it word for word.

JESSICA'S TIP — x

Ask your professor if there's a supplement they would recommend for the course.

Now you might be thinking, I do not have time in my life to read one more thing, I have to figure out what these case rules are for my assigned reading! Supplements are a great way to bolster your understanding because they walk through the material by topic, putting together the rules from the cases for that area. Unlike a textbook that is full of cases, a supplement is best used when it is read after you have already finished your reading for the week to solidify your understanding.

A note of caution: A supplement may include cases not covered in your material. Professors tend to test only on the material taught in the course, so learning material not taught in your course may end up confusing you on an assessment. It is important to wait to read the supplement until after you have an understanding of the assigned cases and material for your course.

SARAH'S TIP — x

I use my supplements to study the topics, but I don't read supplements sequentially. Usually supplements have a table of cases, so I look up the assigned case from my class in the supplement's table of cases and then read each page in the supplement that mentions the case. I do this for each case to make sure I am only bringing into my brain the material applicable to the course. I have limited gray cells, and this helps keep me from learning rules not applicable to the course.

4.4 Outlining

One of the first things you hear about as a study tool is outlining. It is a tried and true method for law school, and it is applicable even within an online format. The key differences are that online students seem to start outlining a bit earlier, and there is less access to past students to get input and templates to work from.

The best outlines are one that you create yourself or with a study group. You are synthesizing the information yourself, and you are guaranteed to only be looking at information from your class and formatting it the way your professor has presented the material. It allows you to build an understanding of how concepts link together, as well as where the concepts may have overlap. For example, in torts, transferred intent applies to several different intentional torts, which allows you to place that section under intent for each section. Additionally, you can include all your course's cases within the outline to give a quick example of the concept in practice.

There is no wrong way to format an outline, but doing flashcards alone will not be enough. Take the information from the flashcards and put it into an outline or a mind map to see how the concepts connect. If you learn by using flashcards, you will still want to make them, but do not rely on flashcards alone to see how topics connect with each other. Some of the most common formats are:

- Traditional Outlines (I, II, A, B, 1, 2)
- Mind Maps
- Flow Charts (can be built into an outline too)
- Grids/Spreadsheets

4.4.1 Traditional Outlines

Traditional outlines can be either bullet points or numbered, with each line indented under an appropriate heading. These can be handwritten or typed. The main advantage of a typed outline is that you can copy and paste repetitive information into the outline, while a handwritten outline needs a little bit more preplanning if later topics need to be added into sections that are already written. When it comes time to make an "attack outline," a short one or two page outline, a typed document is easy to edit down.

Figure 4.1. Tort Outline Sample

Torts

- Generally common law
- Break into elements
- Pay attention to conjunctions (i.e. AND, OR)
- Privileges = defenses; special circumstances allow otherwise prohibited activities.

1. Respondeat Superior
    a. A form of vicarious liability that can be applied to a tort
    b. Requirements:
        i. Person acting within scope of employment
            1. Work assigned by employer
            2. Conduct subject to employer's control
        ii. Not within scope of liability:
            1. Person acting independent of his job
    c. Grant v. Stop-N-Go Market: false imprisonment that the owner was included in the suit because the manager was performing a job duty.

Intentional Torts

I. Personal Torts
    A. Battery
        1. Elements:
            1. Bodily contact (direct or indirect)—touch or strike a person or something intimately connected to the person
                - Direct-the actual person

Figure 4.2. Tort Mind Map Sample

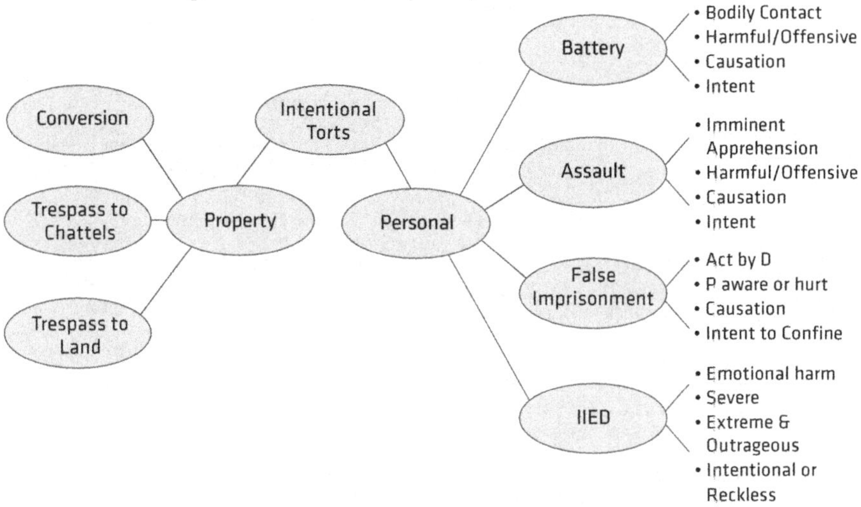

Handwriting the outline is not the end of the world if you retain information best when you write by hand. If you prefer to write it, leave space between each section or even every line/bullet point so that you can add in related information later. Remember, students once made outlines without having a computer and were able to be successful, so you can be too.

BETHANY'S ADVICE — x

Play with the settings on your outline. You want ¼" borders instead of an inch? What about a green background? There are no rules and no requirements that Times New Roman size 12 font has to be the baseline. The more visually interesting you make your outline, the more likely you are to spend time with it and remember visual ques. Of course, there is a balance—there is only so much space to put cute pictures of cats studying the law. However, adding a few elements that engage you with the material can make all the difference in wanting to spend an extra few minutes with the document when studying.

4.4.2 Mind Maps

These may also be referred to as information webs. The basic topic will be in the center, with nodes coming off of it. This is helpful for visual learners.

Figure 4.3. Contracts Flow Chart Sample

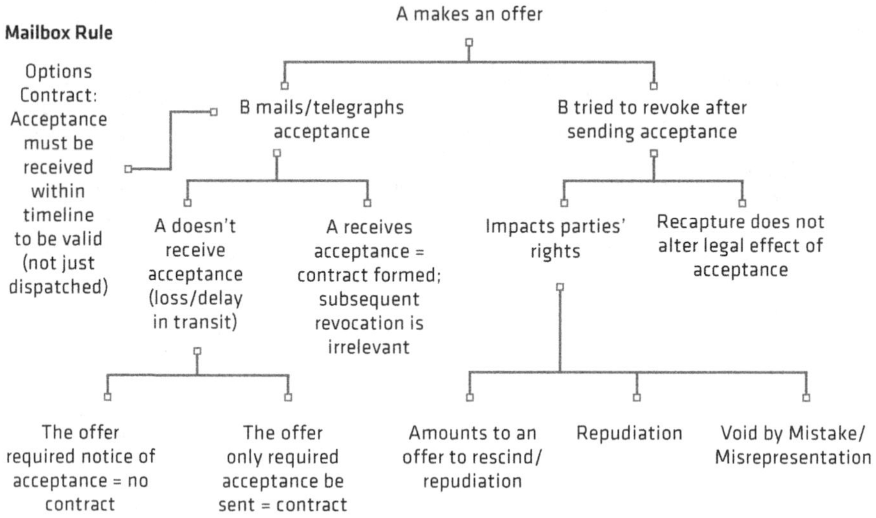

For example: the center may start with torts, with lines branching off to intentional torts and negligence. From intentional torts, it would break down into torts against a person or torts against property. From against a person it would branch to battery, assault, and false imprisonment. From each of them, elements, defenses, and other relevant information would branch off. Mind maps can be very extensive, although they generally are a little harder to print since they can be very large and have many complex branches for each topic.

4.4.3 Flow Charts

Similar to mind maps, a flow chart will direct you from area to area within a rule. This can be helpful if you must follow a particular process every time to get to an accurate result. You can create a flow chart for the class as a whole, or for specific sections that have very detailed procedures.

4.4.4 Grids/Spreadsheets

Like flow charts, a grid can stand alone or be embedded into another format. In a class where cases must be referenced by name, a grid can be an easy way to break down the key components: case name, year, topic, key facts, holding, and rules. This format can be especially helpful for open book exams where the professor has expressed a preference for case names.

Figure 4.4. Intellectual Property Grid Sample

Topic		**Case Name**	**What happened**	**Holding**	**Main rule(s)**
Intro		*Baker v. Selden*	Accounting Method Book dispute	For D. Other parties can reproduce a system of art or science	A © doesn't give the right to limit the use of an art or science explained in it. A patent is necessary to limit use.
		Trademark Cases: United States v. Steffens; United States v. Wittemann; United States v. Johnson	Criminal cases re: TM infringement	Congress has the ability to regulate TMs.	TM exhaust under Common Law, and allow civil actions for damages TMs are the use of a distinctive symbol over time to brand/market TMs fall under Interstate Commerce
		International News Service v. Associated Press	INS reprinting AP's WWI news from France in western markets	Unfair competition when a party takes the work of the other for profit. If it's a tip that's investigated, it's OK.	As competitors, it is unfair competition for a competitor to take the work of another for profit.
TM	Nature & Function	*William R. Warner & Co. v. Eli Lilly & Co.*	Chocolate quinine medicine mix that is very similar in mix and name	A company must sell product as its own, but name can be descriptive	A name that is descriptive of ingredients, qualities, or characteristics cannot become a trademark A company must sell a product as its own, not as if its a competitor's product

The content in your outline is ultimately based on what you need and want, but generally you will want to include any relevant information. The outline generally will include each topic, its elements/factors, defenses, exceptions, and related cases. For the cases, you do not need a lot of information: a few words for the key facts, the holding, the rule, and if it is not under a topic heading, the topic the case relates to. Your initial outline may be over a hundred pages, depending on what you feel is necessary to include.

If you are struggling with an organizational format for your outline, consider looking at the table of contents in your textbook or the topics listed on your syllabus. This will often give you point headings, and can even direct you towards what a case was focusing on for a rule.

You can begin outlining at any time during the semester, although online students tend to prefer starting early because of their other commitments. A weekly or bi-weekly format allows you to cover the material while it is still somewhat fresh in your head, and may allow for better long-term retention. Some students will do it the same week the material is covered in class, while others prefer to wait a week so it has more of a review feeling. When you outline in this way, there is ample time to catch up if you cannot outline in any given week.

Some people may prefer to bulk outline, with large cramming sessions immediately before an assessment, midterm, or final. This may seem effective for retaining information for the specified exam, but remember long-term retention will be key and make life easier when preparing for the bar in a few years. A big drawback to bulk outlining is that you need a devoted large chunk of time in order to sift through all the material. When you have multiple finals for the semester, outlining in this way may not be effective or feasible. There is very little safety net if something comes up for you to complete the outline and effectively study.

If you are in a pinch, there are commercial outlines or outlines from other students that can help give you a guide. We do not recommend these because they may not cover the same material your class covered. Despite this, they can be used to help provide clarity on an issue that you are struggling with. Of the two, an outline from a past student using the same textbook would be preferable over a commercial outline. There is also the added benefit of being able to talk to that student for additional clarity or help if you are struggling.

At the end of the semester you will make your attack outline from the outline you have been preparing all semester. Your attack outline will be a one or two page document that captures the key points from the semester. That one or two page document may have smaller than normal fonts, thin margins, and smaller indents than you are used to. It will not have every piece of information you have learned, just the key information necessary to jog your memory. This attack outline can be used as your study guide. During the refining process you will be able to determine if you have weak areas that you need to review further.

In either the main outline, or based on the key topics of your attack outline, you can also template your exam answers. Since every exam essay will be answered in either an IRAC or CRAC format, you know that you will need a rule statement. By prewriting the rule, you are not only studying, but starting to commit the rule to memory.

If you have an open book exam, you will likely want to reduce your outline to somewhere between 10–20 pages, detailed enough to access information you may need, but not so thick that you cannot reasonably access the information during an exam. This shortened outline should be stapled or in a binder so you do not lose the order by accident during an exam.

JESSICA'S TIP — x

Take a few moments to format your outline document before printing it. It helps having the topic/class and page numbers on the document so you do not accidentally mix up outlines, and you can reorganize them easily if they come out of order.

BETHANY'S TIP — x

I also maintain a running table of cases for any courses that are heavy on case law. My basic chart includes the topic the case falls under, the case name, a short phrase on what it was about, the holding, and what is the rule to take from it. This allows me a quick reference when studying for larger exams when there are close to 150 cases per course.

4.5 Templating

Templating can be a little intimidating to start, but it can be a great study method. Templating is essentially taking the rule statements from your outline and writing them exactly as you would in an essay.

Here is a snippet of the outline example above:

1. Respondeat Superior
    a. A form of vicarious liability that can be applied to a tort
    b. Requirements:
        i. Person acting within scope of employment
            1. Work assigned by employer
            2. Conduct subject to employer's control
        ii. Not within scope of liability:
            1. Person acting independent of his job
    c. Grant v. Stop-N-Go Market: false imprisonment that the owner was included in the suit because the manager was performing a job duty.

If you are templating this section, it may look something like this:

> Respondeat superior is a form of vicarious liability applicable to tort actions. In order to prevail on a respondeat superior theory, a plaintiff must prove by a preponderance of the evidence that the employee was acting within the scope of their employment. The plaintiff can establish the employee was acting within the scope of their employment by demonstrating the employee was performing work assigned by the employer or work that was subject to the employer's control; however, if the employee was acting independent of job duties then the employer is not subject to liability under respondeat superior.

One of the benefits to templating is that you already know exactly how to draft your rule statements during an essay and you are not wasting time trying to figure out how to translate your knowledge from outline format into written sentences. It can be a little difficult to get started with templating in the abstract, so you might find it helpful to start with some essay practice based on hypos (short for hypothetical). Here is an example hypo:

> An employee was following the instructions of their manager when they drove a forklift into a shelf causing items to fall. A box of cat litter fell onto the plaintiff's head. Is the employer likely to be held liable?

Having a concrete hypo to start from can make getting started with templating a little easier. Once you have done a few, you will start to recognize the rules that are universal to the topic and the sub-rules that you would include for a specific circumstance. It is also a great way to test your learning to make sure you understand how to formulate the concepts from your outline into coherent writing. As a reminder, the examples above are simplified student answers. There are likely many more sub-rules and perhaps more exacting language from a case or Restatement introduced in your doctrinal course!

SARAH'S TIP — x

Templating is my favorite method because it forces me to reduce my learnings to writing. I am always more confident if I have been able to template through each of the core topics likely to pop up on an exam essay. Once I started using this method regularly, I was able to quickly develop templates without needing a hypo for inspiration to get started. Sometimes I keep my templates as an entirely separate document, other times I put my template right into my outline.

4.6 Flashcards & Other Study Methods

You have heard plenty about outlining, but can you still use the other methods that have worked for you in the past? YES! But be warned, none of the other methods should be a standalone and you will still want to create an outline.

Flashcards are still a viable and useful study method. There are sources to create digital flashcards, or you can make traditional paper flashcards.

You can use the cards to detail rules, cases, tests, or to have practice questions. For some people, the simple act of handwriting the flashcards can help commit the details to memory. Flashcards are also a great method for self-testing and repetition. Despite this, flashcards alone generally will not show the detailed relationships between concepts, which is the reason an outline is still desirable.

Another popular study method is to create audio files going over key concepts or to rewatch/relisten to recorded lessons, both synchronous and asynchronous. For auditory learners, these are great methods and can even be listened to in downtime, like driving or right before bed.

Key Takeaways

- Brief your cases each week.
- Memorize the black letter law for your doctrinal courses.
- Try different study methods, from traditional outlining or flashcards to more modern tools, to find what works the best for your learning style for that particular course.
- Check out the Appendix for sample student outlines and templates to get a feel for the end product you are working towards.

▷▷▷ 5

Foundations of Survival

5.1 Creating Your Space

Have you considered where you will be doing your studying and class time? For many, the obvious answer is wherever you have room, quiet, or a preexisting office. Many of our classmates built or repurposed unused areas in their homes for these purposes.

Remember if you have options, it is OK to change your location, even if it can be frustrating and time consuming. Figure out what you need and want from your office. You will be spending a lot of time in the space so make it work for you.

Maybe you had been spending a lot of time outdoors prior to starting school, and now you are living inside. Try making sure you have an office space with a window. Natural sunlight can really improve your mood, especially if you are used to getting it and suddenly do not because you are now hidden away in your basement. If you are in an area that has a lot of noise and you find that distracting, try to sound proof it. You never know when that innocuous water line above you will be turned on and go from invisible to obnoxious as you listen to water rush through it and out your hose. A window behind your camera or monitor can be a huge distraction when people are going past or plants are blowing. Consider covering the window with a curtain or paper.

JESSICA'S STORY — x

I have had five different work areas over the course of two years (not including my mobile/outside/travel time). I move around a lot depending on my needs. I do my studying in my upstairs office so I still feel like I am interacting with my family throughout the day, then have class time in my basement office where I can lock out my family from interrupting me.

Adding decorations or colors that help keep you happy and motivated are a plus, especially if you are also working remotely from the area. A picture of your family or a meaningful award or letter (even a negative letter, like your academic probation notice) can be incredibly motivating.

When laying out your work area, consider what you will need in terms of ease and comfort. It might be a rolling chair to move around a large desk. Make sure the materials you use often are easy to access and in a location you can get to without straining. The layout of where things are needs to be easy and intuitive for you, not some idealized layout or Pinterest-worthy picture.

If you need to be distraction-free, consider a lock on your office door. If you have children who are old enough to pick locks, but too young to respect your need for alone time, consider a hasp lock so it can only be secured from inside your area. For significant others or older children, a schedule on the fridge or sign on the door may be sufficient.

And sometimes, you may just need to go to a different area. Your laptop, books, and notebooks are all portable, so changing up your space to fit your needs on any given day is a valid option. You can enjoy the first nice day on your porch after a long winter and still do schoolwork.

BETHANY'S STORY — x

The first year and a half of the program, I had a specific space in our home that was only for law work. I forced myself to work there no matter what to ensure it was distraction-free from work, people, sleeping temptations or otherwise. At first, it worked. Then, I began to feel really sectioned off. I slowly transitioned to allowing myself to take printed materials on car trips, or even out on the back porch. When I let go of the idea that law school should be taken so seriously and separately from everything else in my life, it became much more manageable in terms of stress level. Now I have no hesitations bringing my work with me and only seclude myself when there is a super-strict deadline or something I need a dual monitor for, such as research and writing.

SARAH'S STORY — x

In addition to attending law school remotely, I also work from home. I actually have three different workstations set up and I rotate amongst them to avoid feeling like I am living my entire life in a six square-foot area. Tasks that need the most concentration I do in my office. I tend to rotate stations every two hours or so which is a great breaktime.

5.2 Managing Your Time

Reality check: if you have not previously scheduled out your time, now is the time to start. Law school, especially part-time, and even online, requires a lot of time. You have likely already established some kind of routine prior to your law journey, and may not have needed to schedule things like eating, showering, spending time with a spouse, or even just time away from the computer. They say old habits die hard—do not let this be one of them.

There are a lot of great resources in existence on how to best schedule and utilize said scheduled time. If you have something that is already working for you, then great! We brought together some of the techniques that have worked the best for us in surviving the law school burden, on top of being caregivers, parents, spouses, homeowners, workers, and more.

5.2.1 Schedules

Schedule everything. This might feel like overkill to start; after all, are you taking valuable time to actually schedule time for other things? Yes. And those ten to twenty minutes you spend planning each week just might be the best time spent all week to ensure you have time allotted to everything.

First, get the things that are immovable on your calendar. Are there family gatherings you are required to be part of? Slotted work time that cannot move due to an important meeting with the higher-ups? Probably your class schedule should be here too. Put those down, color code them, and do not move them.

Next, what are those things that need to happen, but are movable as to the time? For example, you know you need to eat, shower, do some homework, etc. Get those things on there, and color code them, too. Be sure to use a different color so your brain knows those can be a bit more flexible. Also, these might be a little less strict in their length of time. You will not know how much homework takes you until you have been in the class. What one week may only be three hours of reading may take you seven hours with a heavier case list. Always schedule extra time in case things take longer than usual.

Then, schedule the fun things, too. Again, utilize a new color. No matter what, make sure there is fun stuff on your schedule every week. We are human and need to take a break. Maybe a date night out, or even just on the couch in another room. Go to a local festival, make a trip to Grandma's.

You should see by now that your schedule is rather booked. Add in your sleep (we all know the suggested eight hours is not always realistic), time set aside for emergencies when your car tire goes flat on the way to work, and, of course, when you have to pick your children up from school when they are sick. What is helpful is that when you have this basic schedule blocked out by color and an emergency arises, you can quickly identify when there is something you can move to another timeslot, or when you will need to call in reinforcements to help so you can maintain certain pieces of your schedule. In the end, your schedule is just that: your schedule. If the colors or boxes do not work for you, that is OK. However, it can be helpful to have a starting point to build off of as you go through your law journey and tweak it for your needs.

There is no shame in asking for help. Going to law school in and of itself is a full-time job, let alone all of the other jobs you are doing on top of it. Whether a friend, a parent, a neighbor—find people you can count on and lean on in times when there just is a bit too much on your plate. And sometimes, that means that homework might not get done. That is OK, too.

BETHANY'S TIP — x

Personally, I use both Google calendar and a paper agenda to schedule my time. My Google calendar I use so I can schedule group projects, as well as communicate to my work colleagues when I am busy versus available. My paper agenda, however, is used as a smaller task manager where I can check off assignments and readings as I go along. This paper agenda helps me keep a physical idea of how much I've completed for the week, as well as try to plan out how much block time I need to set for the various subjects in the coming weeks.

Figure 5.1. Bethany's Agenda

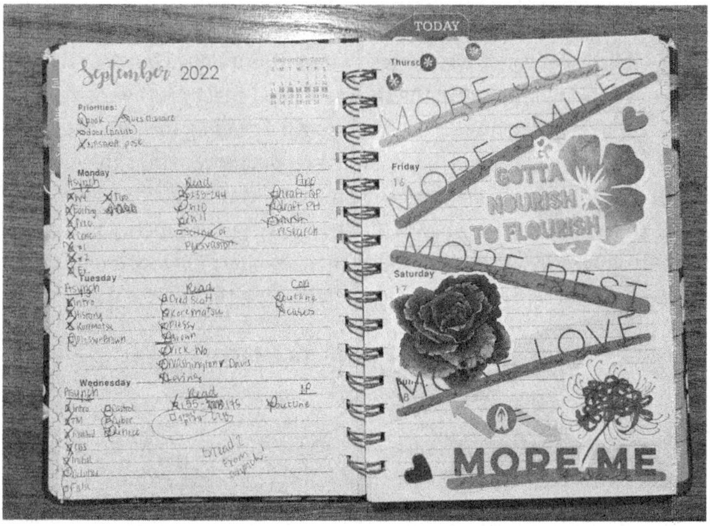

As you'll notice, I separate out my personal goals at the top of the page, then have a day for each subject. Under each subject, I've sectioned out asynchronous work versus reading material versus project work. This helps me plan ahead to see what things are mobile that I can take with me to work on during lunch hour at work or at the in-laws, and what projects are strictly online that require wifi access and specific logins from home. Also notice that there were some things I just ran out of time to read and I made a note so I know to go back later in a future week when I have time to revisit the material I missed.

On the right side, I set aside twenty minutes a week to sticker journal for personal goals for the week. I spend time reflecting on what I need most that week, and set a plan to achieve them. I didn't start this part until my second year of the program, but I have seen a huge improvement in my personal life since starting this practice.

SARAH'S TIP

I found making a weekly to-do list to be a distraction and it was super inefficient for me since the coursework typically requires the same general tasks each week. I make these semester checklists at the beginning of the term to capture all of the work for each class. I have this mapped out for each of the 12 weeks of assigned work in the semester and I check off the corresponding week. For example, once I finish the assigned reading for the first week of Civil Procedure, I cross out the "1" in the reading row. I print this out and it sits on my desk the whole semester so I can always see at a glance where I am at and what I need to do next. I also pencil in a few professional goals on the bottom of my semester checklist to make sure I am continuing to move in the right direction each semester with my long term career goals.

Figure 5.2. Sarah's Template

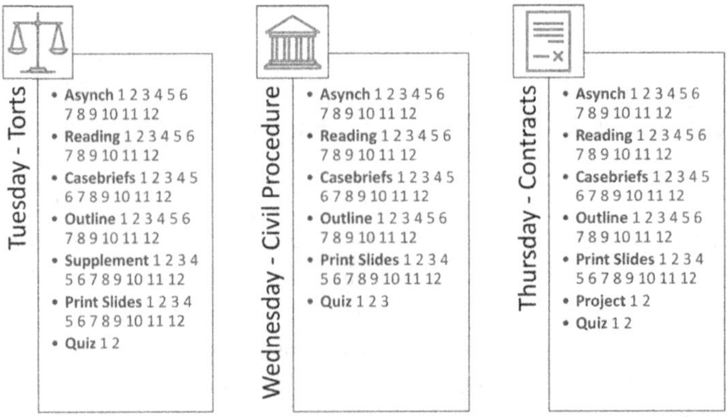

I also print a calendar and it's paper clipped to my semester checklist. I have each of the quiz dates, midterms, project due dates, and finals dates listed out on the calendar. These two pieces of paper are critical to my academic success each semester.

My day to day schedule is broken up into time blocks for work, study time, family time, and eating at designated intervals throughout. I have to designate time for each category to be intentional about ensuring I am operating at peak productivity. I try to observe the Sabbath so I have a pretty full schedule the other 6 days per week. Though transparently, I end up working through some Sabbaths.

5.3 Techniques

Now you have set your time aside, but what do you do to stay focused and actually get the work done that you have been wanting to accomplish? And honestly, what does setting aside time to "study" actually mean?

A great technique is utilizing the Pomodoro or deep work technique. This means taking your large block you have set aside as an hour or so and breaking it into focused chunks. Perhaps the first 25 minutes is spent on case briefing, a five minute break, 20 minutes on asynchronous work, then 5 minutes outlining, followed by another break. Usually this is done on a four cycle rotation with a longer break, but the reality is finding what works best for you. Those minutes seem to fly by, as compared to setting longer goals of just focusing on material until you're done with the subject. Having shorter, action-oriented goals help to accomplish more!

Another technique is mirroring. This is especially great for those of us in online programs. Schedule a Zoom time where you and at least one other classmate have to get things done. Set a timer, mute yourselves, and get to work. What we love about this is that being in a setting where others are also working helps us to also focus on getting things done. Even better, when you get to something you have a question on, you do not have to wait for a response in a groupme or other messaging app, but can unmute and ask then and there. Even if it's not with another classmate, try this with a child or a spouse. While they are working on paying the bills or their school work, you can focus on your own.

Lastly, a great technique is also finding ways to delegate or lessen the load on tasks. Obviously, you cannot delegate your coursework—that would be academic dishonesty and we want to be very clear it is not a good path to take. Outside of that, there are other ways to make use of this technique. Mowing the grass takes a long time? Hire a company. It makes a great holiday/birthday gift from those who love you. If money is a concern, then turn it into a study game: can you memorize all five elements within one outline of the yard? Not enough time to cook dinner? Purchase a meal planning kit that delivers to your door. Many times they cost just about the same as your weekly shopping kits, and yet they save you time and brain power by picking the meals and pre-cutting the vegetables. Deciding on date night takes so long that the dates themselves are cut short? Do a quick social media request asking friends and families to send you note cards with date ideas—with bonus points for sending gift cards with their ideas!

Find what works for you, and keep an open mind when you learn about other ways your classmates have found to survive the mounting responsibilities. Balancing an online life in law school with a physical life at home and even work is a lot. It does not hurt to try something once. The best case: it works for you and your life is easier. The worst case: you have checked off one more thing on the list of what does not work for you.

5.4 The Playing Field

It may not feel like you have entered a level playing field. There are likely going to be classmates that seem like they have less on their plate to juggle than the massive load you have found yourself with. It is real. Some students may not be working full-time, or they may not have the same family dynamics such as children or spouses. Whatever your circumstances are in relation to your peers, know that you do not have to be the same to have the same opportunity for strong academic outcomes. We have found it is best to focus on your individual journey rather than comparing workloads.

Those with prior legal experience seem to already have background knowledge, which is great for acclimating to online legal learning. If this is you, congratulations—you may have a leg up on your peers. A word of caution, we have often heard this advantage is narrowly construed to the first semester and that after that those without a legal background prior to law school seem to be on a level playing field. If it seems like you are leading the pack at the beginning, do not get complacent with having a lead. We have all seen the races where the front runner is lax and ends up surpassed. If you do not have prior legal experience and it seems like everybody that does is so far ahead, just focus on learning your first semester and you will catch right up.

5.5 Accommodations

Wait! Before you skip this section thinking it does not apply to you, do not turn that page just yet.

There are two sides to accommodations in law school: those legally granted to you for physical, mental, psychological, learning, or other reasons under the ADA, and those granted to you out of the kindness of your professor's (or program's) heart. Whether you have previously been granted an accommodation prior to law school or not, the reality is that life happens, and you might need one.

5.5.1 Legal Accommodations

If you had a 504 or IEP in high school, you may have already known to start this process. If we had to narrow it down to a single most important piece of advice for you, we would suggest that you start the process as soon as you accept enrollment. Oops... If you are not reading this book that early, no better time than to start now, right?

Legally, academic institutions are required to provide reasonable accommodations to their students with proper documentation. If you are interested in the law for this, be sure to review the Americans with Disabilities Act (ADA). Some programs follow the MPRE guidelines for documentation, but not all do. Be sure to check with your institution to learn the process, timeline, and requirements if this is something you are interested in pursuing.

Second strongest piece of advice: if you can have accommodations, and need them, use them. For some reason, there is a lot of pride in academia for not using accommodations. Do not let pride be the reason you struggle. Common accommodations include extended time, access to calming items, receiving materials ahead of time, and even adaptation of the in-person hours requirements. You do not want to be in a place where you need them and cannot use them.

If you are struggling, and think it might be a potential difference in ability, we encourage you to pursue getting tested. Many law students are innately smart and are able to mask differing abilities throughout prior academic journeys. It is never too late to pursue this avenue.

AUTHOR STORY — x

I started the accommodation process during the first week of the semester, and the soonest the department overseeing the requests could get me in for the initial meeting was nearly 20 days. There are time limits for requesting accommodations that could hinder your access to them in any given semester. Know the requirements for your institution and be sure to double check them each semester as they may change!

5.5.2 Other Life Necessities

Law school has a connotation of being very cold and strict. And, for better or worse, it largely is.

Luckily, the instructors are also human and usually have empathy for the students they teach. Why does this matter? Because you, too, are human.

There will be points in your program where things come up. We advise that you try to plan as much as possible around class times and projects, but the reality is that life happens. You may have planned a wedding before you learned your class assignments, have an unexpected trip to the ER, or even have a sick child you need to care for. It is OK to share your humanity and ask for accommodation from your professor even though it is not a legally covered reason under the ADA.

Your professor may very well say "no." Be prepared for that: if that is your answer, have things in place. Either take the zero or push through it. Sometimes an extension just is not feasible due to the flow of the course, professor needs, or program requirements. In this case, even a partially completed assignment is better than none.

In our experience, however, most professors will be willing to work with you. But, that comes with a price. When you make the ask, be honest, explain why you need the accommodation, be specific, and provide a potential solution. If you are missing class, how can you make up that time? If you need an extension on a project, how can you make sure this is not harming the progression of your colleagues? Most importantly, when it is accepted: hold up your end of the bargain! There is nothing worse than turning in a half-completed assignment after advocating for your work and a new timeline.

BETHANY'S STORY

I was one of those folks who needed an extension not covered under the ADA. Due to COVID, my honeymoon was rescheduled two years into the program. School is important, but I wasn't about to give up such an important event. I managed to purchase wifi on the ship, and with my camera off, was still able to attend the classes, 3am honeymoon time. Unfortunately, the pre-recorded videos I needed for the midterm took too much bandwidth for the wifi access available. In a panic, I reached out to the professor, explaining the situation, and was granted a week-long extension to allow me to return to the country and prepare the material. The moral of this story is communication! I communicated to all of my professors prior to the semester starting, the week of, and the day of to ensure if anything went funky, that they had a background of what was happening and why.

5.6 Study Groups

We each have our own approach to study groups, but all of us agree having them in some format is helpful. If nothing else, we encourage you to give study groups the good "law school try" before deciding what is the best option for you moving forward.

5.6.1 Jessica's Study Group Suggestions

My first semester I was in a very rigid study group with four other people. We met once a week after class and had very specific criteria to prepare for the week. It worked, even if sometimes it was hard to find the time to get the prep work done. This group had great people in it, but that does not mean this was necessarily the best for my study style and the personalities were not a great match. We lasted one semester.

Despite not creating a long term group, I did learn a lot. First, I learned the value of cooperative study. Only one time during undergrad did I try to join a study group, and it was a terrible experience. I was incredibly hesitant to have a study group, but having set expectations was great. We also spent a lot of time creating hypotheticals for essay style discussion as well as multiple choice. It reinforced concepts like red herrings, and the fact that people may approach scenarios differently. Creating the hypotheticals and trying to predict how the others in the group might approach the issue helped expand my understanding of different topics.

Never underestimate the importance of a classmate's analysis. In practice you will need to think outside the box, so seeing what issues others consider will help broaden your view of an issue as well. Remember, in a case both sides argue valid points, so there is no one right answer. The same can be said during an exam. There may be a stronger side, but if you can effectively argue your point, you will not get a zero.

Since then, my study groups have been more on an as-needed basis. It fits my schedule more realistically. We generally meet for several sessions right before exams, and there is nothing wrong with studying in this manner if that is what works for your schedule. We also create group outlines or documents, as well as our own, which we share amongst each other. Sometimes seeing the different approaches people take, even on paper, can be helpful.

5.6.2 Bethany's Study Group Suggestions

If it was not for my first study group, I would not have survived the first year. We called ourselves the Three Amigos and formed by the end of the first semester. I learned a lot in this group that I was able to take with me into other groups that really and truly were the foundation of my success in the program. By the end of the semester you might find that you have not joined just a study group, but a support group.

Be up front with what you need out of the group. No one can read your mind: communicate! Set expectations early of what you are wanting to achieve within the group, how often you are wanting to meet, and what everyone is responsible for when it comes to shared documents. Some semesters you will have the time and brain space to meet weekly, while others you are only meeting before big tests. If you are working on a joint outline, how often do you expect everyone to update it? Setting these early will prevent many awkward conversations later.

Be flexible. Chances are, not everyone in the group studies the exact same way. Be open to trying new methods of outlining, practicing multiple choice, and sharing sources. Share your way of studying, learn someone else's way, then see if you can merge the formats together. The more ways you review the information, the better off you both will be.

Make it about more than just "studying." Sometimes to get to the studying part, you need to get through the humanity part first. Sometimes that means venting about a quiz after the quiet period is over, or maybe just talking about the silly thing that happened at work that day. Just be sure to make space for life, but set a limit so it is not overshadowing your entire time. Identify a time to be started on the materials, and allot additional time post-studying for continuing those conversations if needed. For us, having scheduled time specifically for catching up was beneficial to help with balancing the time.

It is OK to have more than one. You are not cheating on a study group by meeting with more than one of them. The reality is that things change. Eventually, your group may dissolve, colleagues may take different classes or change their minds about law school, or maybe they just find that way of studying does not work for them or their schedules. Having many options to study also helps to maximize your understanding of the material. Personally, I have four main study groups that I frequent, and have a handful of colleagues that I study with one on one when the opportunity presents itself. By diversifying who I am studying with, I have learned many new studying methods and have been able to connect and network with more colleagues. Plus, it can be fun to create names and form these new supportive bonds. Just a quick shout out to all of my study groups for being such an important piece of my law journey!

5.6.3 Sarah's Study Group Suggestions

I have the unpopular opinion that does not really comport with the typical advice: I do not really get a lot out of study groups from an academic perspective. There, I said it. I prefer to study solo because it is easier for me to make sure I am grasping the materials. I usually only attend a couple of study groups per semester, and there are some classes that I did not attend a single session. I got CALI's in those classes.

What does work really well for me is making sure I grasp the material. I really enjoy asynchronous study groups where we share outlines and issue spotting documents through joint documents when it works for our lives. Even if a study group is doing a group outline, I always do my own because the group outlines do not really work for my own memorization. After I have made my outline, I look for the group outline and try to identify gaps to help support the group.

When I do attend study group sessions, I prefer to have already mastered the material. I try to help others understand the concepts if there is something they are still struggling with. A great analogy is the infamous airline directions before takeoff—it works best for me to make sure I have my own mask on and then help those around me with their masks. This aspect of study groups is helpful because it is a great way to ensure I understand the material. If I am unable to explain a concept to someone else, then I am not ready to write an exam essay about the topic.

The biggest benefit for me in study groups is the social connection. There is something amazing about connecting with others that have the shared experience of law school because there are some tough days and crazy life curveballs. I have developed deep connections with classmates through the shared experience of law school and some lifelong friends (fingers crossed). That said, connecting socially at the beginning of a study group should be kept to a minimum because classmates need to use that time for productivity. I tend to message with the members of my study groups often, but am generally solo throughout the semester in terms of academic study efforts.

I wish someone had told me in the first semester of law school that study groups do not work for everyone. It seemed like all the advice I encountered indicated studying with peers was a necessity for a successful law school journey. Making connections with your peers is important, but you can excel in law school even if your style is independent study. I think the key for me is seeking out model answers that differ from my own analysis to help become well-rounded in my thought process and approach. As long as you are intentional about taking a holistic perspective, you can thrive with a solo study strategy.

5.7 Office Hours

10 out of 10 recommend going to office hours.

You may never have attended an office hour session in undergrad (or other graduate studies if applicable), but law school is different. Some professors hold weekly office hours and others will schedule with students upon request. This is prime time for asking questions or listening to other students' questions. These sessions are generally filled with nuggets of wisdom that you need for your final, the bar, and are even helpful for practice.

You may be thinking, there is no time in my life to pack in one more thing! We feel that deeply and you are not alone. If you are not able to attend office hours, double check to see if there is a recording. More often than not, we learn more from listening to the responses to other students' questions than the answers to the questions we were wondering about. You can listen to the recording any time of the day or even as you fall asleep at night.

If you need to be strategic about your schedule, attending office hours right before midterms and finals is where you will likely get the biggest bang for your buck. Also, coming prepared with a list of questions will also help you get the most out of office hours. By forcing yourself to write down your questions in advance, you have necessarily thought through the material enough to identify your knowledge gaps. Figuring out what you do not know or understand is a huge step forward in the learning process.

Attending an office hour session gives you a chance to learn about your professor on a deeper level and build connections with them in a smaller setting. Your professors are people, actual human beings with lives of their own and likely a rich practice area. They may be teaching a basic doctrinal course, but their expertise is far greater. Even though it may not feel like it in class with the Socratic method, professors actually do like students and enjoy educating the next generation of lawyers.

BETHANY'S TIP — x

Office hours don't always work for your schedule. Asking if the instructors are willing to record the session for those unable to be in attendance can be helpful. Additionally, office hours are usually not limited to just set hours. If you have pressing questions that don't fit concisely into an email, there is nothing stopping you from reaching out to a professor to see about a small group office hour. Sometimes these smaller opportunities to meet with the professor allow for greater depth and conversation on a topic. Just remember that this time is valuable and be prepared so you are not taking up more time than you need.

Key Takeaways

- Set up your study space to thrive.
- Diligently plan your schedule.
- Explore the possibility of accommodations.
- Join or launch a study group.
- Attend office hours whenever possible.

▷▷▷ 6

Mastering Multiple Choice

Law school: home of the phrase "it depends." Except, when it does not actually "depend."

Although you will be faced with many opportunities to throw spaghetti at the wall and hope it sticks (i.e., writing essays and debating the gray zone of what you are trying to prove), you are also likely to be faced with your fair share of multiple choice questions. A unique feature of law school multiple choice questions is the concept of the "best answer." This means there can actually be more than one right answer, but your job is to find the best of the right answers. In this style of question, there **is** a right and wrong answer.

Most multiple choice questions are used to test your knowledge of the rules. A final exam may have one to five essay questions and it would be very difficult for your professor to write an exam question to cover the breadth of rules taught in the course. Accordingly, the essays usually focus on key concepts and the multiple choice questions allow the professor to drill into your knowledge of a broader array of rules. The key to doing well on multiple choice questions is to focus on learning the rules.

SARAH'S TIP — x

One of the things that I had to realize about multiple choice questions is they aren't asking what I think about the question—hang with me on this one. The light bulb went off during torts when I got a practice multiple choice question incorrect. It was about a 12-year-old ninja trick-or-treater and whether or not there was reasonable apprehension based on the conduct. My thought process was that 12-year-olds are generally about my height, it was dark, and I've seen too many movies to think every person that comes to your door on Halloween has good intentions. So I answered the question from my subjective viewpoint. But here's the thing: it doesn't matter if I would have felt scared by the trick-or-treater, what mattered was the fact pattern indicated the trick-or-treater had displayed the same conduct at the previous eight houses and none of those home occupants had been fearful because it was Halloween and kids dress up in ninja costumes and come to your door. As you're navigating multiple choice questions, try to remember it's simply a time for you to display your knowledge of the rules.

Why do these even matter? Because many of you are likely to take a bar exam, which will include some kind of multiple choice questioning. Previously there has been a six-hour exam with 200 multiple choice questions that accounts for 50% of your score. Because multiple choice questions have been heavily bar tested, professors tend to include them on exams as well. So yes, multiple choice questions are an important piece of your law school experience.

Multiple choice questions can be formulated in a variety of ways. The most common style of multiple choice questions on law school exams are multiple choice questions with four possible answers (for the sake of demonstration some of the examples listed below have been simplified and shortened). Our goal is to prepare you for approaching different styles of questions and not teaching doctrinal concepts—we will save that pleasure for your professors! Without further ado, some scenarios to be prepared for include:

6.1 Multiple Choice Basics

Common law systems create the possibility of courts expanding and narrowing the rule over time, which means it is very likely there might be multiple correct elements. Be sure to slow down and read all of the potential options as more than one could be correct.

- EX: The Defendant punched the Plaintiff in the face, breaking the Plaintiff's nose, because the Plaintiff insulted the Defendant's prized flower pot.

A. Yes, because the Defendant touched the Plaintiff.
B. Yes, because the Defendant intentionally made contact with the Plaintiff's face, breaking the Plaintiff's nose, by using the Defendant's fist to punch the plaintiff.

If you have not covered the tort of battery yet, here is a quick rundown of the elements: the defendant acts intentionally, causing harmful or offensive contact to the Plaintiff. While answer A includes touch, which is similar to contact, it is not the best answer because answer B uses the term of art "contact" from the rule and also includes the other elements from the rule. This is an example where there is clearly a better answer.

Hinging on a singular word difference: These questions usually hinge on connecting words such as "but," "and," or "or." Take time to circle these words (or highlight when using a digital exam software) to help you focus on the main rule and elements.

- EX: The Plaintiff was aware of being confined in the library, but the Plaintiff was not harmed by the defendant's intentional confinement. Is the Plaintiff likely to recover for false imprisonment?
  A. Yes, because the Plaintiff was aware of the defendant's confinement.
  B. No, because the Plaintiff was not harmed by the defendant's confinement.

You may not have covered the tort of false imprisonment yet, but one of the elements requires the Plaintiff is aware of OR harmed by the confinement. Here, because the Plaintiff was aware of the confinement, the lack of harm will not be a barrier to recovery because only one OR the other is required. As the Plaintiff was aware of the confinement, thereby satisfying the element of false imprisonment, the best answer here is Answer A.

Which statement is TRUE/FALSE: These questions will ask for you to pick the statement that is either true or false. The questions are especially confusing since you are reading mostly the opposite of what you are looking for and you may second guess yourself. These questions may have double negatives to add additional confusion.

- EX: Which of the following statements are true:
  A. Bilateral contract formation requires mutual assent.
  B. Grass is usually blue.
  C. The sky is almost always orange.
  D. Leaves tend to fall off trees in the springtime.

  Even if you have not studied contracts formation, you could probably still find the right answer to this question. It is likely because you were able to eliminate the last three options. This is a valuable tool in approaching multiple choice questions, because you can effectively use the process of elimination and still earn points even if the correct answer is not one that you remembered.

- TIP: Eliminate all the answers that are in common (all true or all false).

Written in the negative: These questions are best read a few times. They are purposely written in the negative to get you to think about the rule in a different way.

- EX: Plaintiff did not not experience emotional distress after being in the zone of danger when the defendant's car negligently struck her mother. Is the plaintiff likely to recover?
  A. The harm is likely sufficient to recover on a claim for negligent infliction of emotional distress.
  B. The harm is likely insufficient to recover on a claim for negligent infliction of emotional distress because the Plaintiff did not experience emotional distress.

  Double negative questions are challenging when you are in a timed setting and trying to move through the material quickly. There are only two possible choices here, and the best answer is Answer A because the double negative in the question means the Plaintiff did experience emotional distress.

- TIP: Sometimes a double negative is used. It is a grammatical trick, so you may need to reword the question in your mind.

Regurgitation of material you have read: These are used fairly often as reading checks for supplemental books or reading that you may not get to in the actual course. Briefing cases and taking notes during your reading can be extremely helpful.

Spanning 2–10+ possible answer choices: This has been a rare sight because reading so many potential answers takes up so much exam time, but be prepared for questions that have potentially up to 10 (or more) answers to choose from, sometimes with only a word or two different from the others. The same methods described above apply to these questions as well, but you may have a few more options to sort through.

- TIP: If the key difference is a single word, use the exam's highlighting feature to help clarify the distinctions between the answers.

True and false: While not nearly as common on exams, this style of question can pop up from time to time. These questions have only two answers and normally are used for a very basic level of understanding of a topic.

Regardless of the style of question, it is important to always read carefully through the call of the question and each answer—even if you read the question, instantly know the answer, look down, and find an answer that is nearly spot on. You do not want to miss a question you would have gotten correct had you taken the time to read through each of the available responses. Some answers may be formatted as "yes, unless . . . ," which can be another level of complexity beyond the format of the question. Slow down and read each response carefully.

You have probably noticed we use words such as "may" and "likely" throughout this book. It is more of a rarity in the legal field to have absolutes because there are so many exceptions and defenses. Accordingly, you should consider responses that include "always" or "never" as red flags. Responses with this strength of verbiage are rarely correct from our experience, so carefully consider each response before selecting one with such firm language.

For some of you, these will be your bread and butter. For others of you, this style of question will be the bane of your existence. Either way, it is important to be prepared and approach these questions in a way that works best for you.

Three Pro Tips:

- Practice. And then do some more practice multiple choice questions. Download an app or two on your phone and practice. Even getting a couple of practice questions in while you are in line to check out from the grocery store or filling up with gas can make a huge difference. Be aware that some of the practice materials may not cover the same issues or rules that your book and professor cover, so outside study materials can sometimes add confusion. If you are repeatedly seeing questions that you are getting wrong, make sure you are not testing on a topic you have not covered yet.

- Always read the explanation for every multiple choice practice question, even if you selected the correct choice. It is invaluable to understand "why" that answer was the correct choice and also "why" the other choices were not correct. This will help boost your success for answering multiple choice questions, but it also gives you exposure to the terms of art and phrasing you will need for your essay writing. Think of this study tip as a two-for-one deal. If you do not understand the rationale after reading it, ask the professor. Make sure you copy the question, answers, and reasoning because without the specifics, the professor may not be able to give you a clear explanation so you can better understand the reasoning.
- You know those pesky pages at the end of each chapter that seem like fluff? Some textbooks have questions at the end of each chapter. Do every single one, even if they are not assigned.

SARAH'S TIP — x

Practice multiple choice questions each week for your doctrinal courses. It helps build your knowledge of the subject matter as you progress through the materials.

6.2 Different Approaches

There are many different ways to approach multiple choice questions. You may find one method is most natural to you, or you may use a variety of techniques depending on the question you encounter. The key is knowing different strategies and finding your own best method of approaching these types of questions.

Prediction

Start by predicting the answer to the question. Once you have read the fact pattern, you should have a general sense of which answer you are looking for. Then look at the answers and select the one that is most closely aligned with your prediction. With this method, it is still a good idea to double check the other answers to make sure you did not miss anything in the analysis.

Gut Reaction

You may need to adopt a rule for yourself with respect to multiple choice questions: never go back and change your answer if you had a strong initial gut feeling after reading the question and answer choices. If you are doing practice questions and notice you end up getting it wrong every time you have changed your answer, try this strategy on your next set of practice questions.

If the gut reaction rule is for you, do not take this as a pass to not to go back and double check your work. Sometimes you rush when you are reading an exam. If you have extra time, make sure that you did not misread the questions, and do not be afraid to change your answer when you realize that you missed a keyword that changes the scenario. Missing words may change the intent or cause of a scenario and can change everything.

Essay It Out

For those of you who seem to do best at essays, this might be the perfect routine for you. Start by reading the question and do not look at the answer choices. Quickly do a mental IRAC in your head. This does not have to be in full sentences or even fully thought out. A bullet-pointed IRAC, if you will, is the perfect length. Then, look at the answer choices and choose the one that most closely aligns with your answer. It probably will not be identical, but chances are you came pretty close to one of them.

Narrowing the Choices

Once you have figured out which rule the multiple choice question is testing, you can usually narrow down the options to two strong contenders. From there, it is a matter of selecting the best of the two remaining options. Take a deep breath, walk yourself through the rules, and then make your selection.

If the exam software has an option to cross out wrong answers, do it! This will assure you that if you go back to check your answer you will not get distracted by clearly wrong answers.

Game the System

There are only so many ways to frame a question to test your knowledge of a specific rule. Once you have gone through a plethora of practice questions, you will be able to recognize which rule a question was written to test on. Your law school likely provides access to several resources of practice questions. The inside scoop is your professors have access to these same materials and often use them as inspiration when writing exams.

Watch for Red Herrings and Focus on the Call of the Question

When you read the call of the question, it may ask for something that you would not necessarily think of because another issue or fact is more prevalent. Make sure the answer you select is answering the question. There will often be an answer that is true, clear, and a valid point, but it is a distraction from the actual question. For example: If a question asks if a property owner can stop a trespasser when there is private necessity, and one of the answers focuses on private necessity requiring a trespasser to pay for any damage to the property, that will not be the right answer if it is not answering the question being asked.

If you have not covered this in torts yet, all you need to know for this next example is trespass requires entry whereas assault requires apprehension of imminent contact. A question may state a property owner can hold the defendant liable when the defendant walked across the property owner's lawn without consent and one of the answers may be "no, because the property owner was not in apprehension of imminent contact from the defendant." While this may be true, it is a rule for assault and not trespass. This type of question likely includes an answer pertaining to liability for trespass because the defendant entered the property without consent.

Other Things to Keep in Mind

There will be times that there is not an answer that stands out to you. It could be the professor wrote the question incorrectly, or perhaps none of the answers is the perfect answer. In these instances, just choose the best answer that is available to choose from. Do not lose out on points because you think there could be a better way to write an answer. (You can show this to them in your essay response.) Remember, a multiple choice question is not focused on what you think of the question; it is a time for you to display you understand which rule is being tested and how to apply the rule to the fact pattern.

Conclusion

The great news is you are unlikely to encounter a multiple choice question in practice. If this style of testing your learning is a struggle, rest assured a judge is not going to predicate the outcome of your client's case on whether you answer A, B, or C. However, practicing finding the best answer does prepare you to frame your client's case in the strongest way.

BETHANY'S STORY — x

I have told my husband on more than one occasion that if a future employer hands me a multiple choice test for an interview, that would be my red flag. I'm one of the folks where multiple choice exams have single-handedly tanked my scores. If my preferred answer isn't on the list, I struggle to find the "best" answer as it usually feels too subjective. I have found the most success when professors allow a space at the end of the exam for students to anonymously argue for why a question could not be effectively answered with the available choices. This allowed professors to see how a question could have been read differently than they had intended. I suggest meeting with your professors often if this is your struggle to learn how they phrase their questions and what they are looking for in their responses.

SARAH'S STORY — x

I was working through the practice problems in the end of the chapter and the textbook answer section indicated each answer could be correct. What?!?! The textbook answer then walked through each answer and how it could be the correct answer. It then gave the "best answer." I knew at that moment that I was in a whole new world and had to figure out how to study for multiple choice questions in this format.

JESSICA'S TIP

During exams, I use all the features available to me. Highlight, cross out answers, and flag anything I am not 100% sure on. If I have time at the end, I go back and check all of the multiple choice questions, paying special attention to the flagged questions. Sometimes another question can help jog your memory on a rule.

Key Takeaways

- On multiple choice questions, there is a best answer, and your job is to find it.
- Practice multiple choice questions, regularly.
- Always double check the call of the question and carefully read each answer before making your selection.
- Take a little time to figure out which strategy, or strategies, work best for you because there is often limited time to answer multiple choice questions on an exam.

▷▷▷ 7

Exemplary Essays

This chapter is pretty much alphabet soup. Spoiler alert, this is also one of the longest chapters. The bar exam includes an essay portion and most law school courses likewise include essays as part of the assessment process. Essays are usually worth the bulk of the available points on an exam and we want to make sure you are set up for success.

There are many different approaches to writing essays, but the key is to understand the big picture. Whether your professor prefers IRAC, CRAC, CRAP, CREXAC, CREAC, or some other awesome combo, they are all fairly similar. We are starting this chapter with the end result in mind to help anchor the concepts.

IRAC: Issue, Rule, Application, Conclusion
CRAC: Conclusion, Rule, Application, Conclusion
CRAP: Conclusion, Rule, Application, Policy
CREXAC: Conclusion, Rule, rule Explanation, eXamples, Application, Conclusion
CREAC: Conclusion, Rule, Explanation, Application, Conclusion

It is important to ask each of your professors which format they prefer and write in that format on the final for their class. This means that you may be writing in different ways for different classes. While this can feel a little overwhelming at first, it prepares you really well for practice because supervising attorneys are going to have their own preferences and you will need to learn to write specific to those as well.

"It depends" is almost always the right answer in law school. No really, it is. This is because there are so many minute details that can change the outcome of the hypothetical. There can be jurisdictional splits that give a variety of answers to explain, plus when juries are added into the mix there is a level of unpredictability that may need to be addressed. Multiple choice questions are written to have a "best answer," but professors often write essay questions that could go either way and it is your job to put forth a strong argument. Some essay questions are written with a clear outcome in mind, and the following materials will help you succeed with either. There is never enough time within an assessment for the essays. The key to performing well is having a framework in mind heading in.

It is also important to frame things in your own words to make sure you understand them. It is also important to use the terms of art to describe the rules in formal writing such as exam essays. This can feel a little overwhelming to balance at first, but you will get the hang of it. If you can explain the legal concept to a second grader, and the second grader can understand it, then you have succeeded. Our role as attorneys is to be able to explain legal concepts to our clients, and within law school our job is to write an essay that demonstrates we know the applicable legal terms of art and that we understand how to explain, using terms of art and our own words, how those rules would be applied to the fact pattern. Clear as mud, right?

7.1 The Basic Format

Issue Spotting

Some suggest that you read the call of the question first and then read the fact pattern. Others suggest skimming the fact pattern, reading the call of the question, and then doing a deep dive reading of the fact pattern. Whichever method you find helps you internalize the material the quickest is the method you will want to use. Understanding the call of the question is critical for your issue spotting and essay formulation. If the call of the question asks you to analyze Plaintiff A's claims, you do not want to write your entire essay describing all of the claims that Plaintiff B can assert.

As you are reading the fact pattern, you will want to "issue spot" along the way. This means you are identifying the legal issues you will need to discuss in your analysis. You should be able to identify what topic the questions are testing you about. Start by jotting down each issue you have identified in the fact pattern. Next you will want to order the issues based upon which ones are the most important to the ones that are least important.

JESSICA'S TIP

A great way to prepare for essay writing is to look at a fact pattern as a study group and try to identify each issue. This is much quicker than group drafting an essay and can also be done asynchronously through a shared document or even via email. You can use commercially available essays and responses. Once everyone in the study group has had a chance to identify the issues, share the model answer and figure out what, if anything, you missed and why you missed it. Going through this process is a great way to start prepping your essay writing skills for a particular course.

SARAH'S TIP

I tend to also include a couple of key facts along with the issue so I can glance at it and recall the fact pattern.

BETHANY'S TIP

As I identify issues, I bring them down into the text box so I remember to include them in my overarching argument. This allows me to do a quick outline and reorder things so they will flow better in the final essay. Especially when this is an everything-and-the-kitchen-sink argument, it allows me to manage time better for any smaller issues. Sometimes that one extra sentence can make the difference of being at the curve or above it.

Some essay prompts are very narrowly focused on a couple of key things to work through and other essays feel like it is everything and the kitchen sink. Either way, your issue spotting should include everything you can find. When in doubt, and this will likely happen, if a cause of action is inapplicable make note of it and why it does not apply.

Issue statements can be written in a couple of different ways in an exam essay. If your professor prefers that you start with the conclusion, draft these as conclusory statements rather than issue statements. If your professor does not state a preference between starting with an issue statement or a conclusory statement, we recommend starting with a conclusory statement. If you run out of time to draft a conclusion at the end of your essay, you have already stated the conclusion to your analysis and will be likely to score more points than if you started with an issue statement and ran out of time to draft a conclusion.

Here are a couple of examples:

> **Issue Statement:** The issue is whether the plaintiff is likely to prevail on a claim for trespass when the defendant intentionally walked across the plaintiff's yard to pick a flower.

> **Conclusory Statement:** A court is likely to find the defendant liable for trespass because the defendant intentionally walked across the plaintiff's yard in order to pick a flower.

Both of these examples set the stage for the analysis by identifying the cause of action to be analyzed, trespass, and the key facts for the elements of trespass.

Rules and Explanations

Once you have your list of issues, start with the most important issue in the fact pattern and draft the rules for the issue. After you have drafted the core rules, you will want to draft the explanations. Even if your professor says to use IRAC or CRAC, the rule explanations are expected to be included as part of the "R" for rules. Here is an example rule statement:

> In order to establish a prima facia claim for negligence, the plaintiff must prove by a preponderance of evidence that the defendant (1) owed a duty of care to the Plaintiff, (2) the defendant breached that duty, (3) the Plaintiff suffered an injury that was (4) caused by the defendant's injury.

- Prima facia—did you know that one or did you go look it up when you came across it? If you are not familiar with the term, take a moment and look it up before continuing.
- The legal standard, by a preponderance of evidence, is included.
- The rule statement indicates which party has the burden of proof, the Plaintiff.

- The elements for the claim, negligence, are clearly drafted.

Next, we'll practice drafting an explanation to support our rule statement. Here is an example of providing an explanation for causation (element 4 listed above):

> To establish causation, the plaintiff must prove the defendant's breach was both the actual cause and the proximate cause of the Plaintiff's injury. Actual cause is determined by the "but for test" under which the plaintiff must establish but for the defendant's breach, the plaintiff would not have been harmed. Proximate cause limits the defendant's liability to foreseeable harm.

These explanatory sentences explain what the plaintiff must demonstrate in order to satisfy the element of causation.

Case Illustrations

Case illustrations are sometimes included as rules explanations because cases help illustrate the application of the rule, essentially providing sub rules. Some professors will expect you to know case names and frame the rule explanation as the court's holding in the case. Additionally, case rules help with the analysis that we will dive into next.

Analysis

Analysis is the crux of your job as a law student and in your role as an attorney someday. You have to be able to take a fact pattern, understand existing case law, and identify the likely outcome of the case.

Any time you make an assertion, it should be supported by your analysis. When in doubt, always include "because" in your sentence. This will force you to explain your analysis by citing back to facts from the fact pattern for each particular point. This will allow you to measure the strength of your assertion and append the appropriate qualifier. This is not an exhaustive list, but gives you an idea of the spectrum:

- Will: Absolutely certain. This should be used sparingly because most fact patterns leave room for debate and you never really know what a jury might do!
  Example: The court will find for the plaintiff.

- Likely: Probably. This should be used if you find there is strong support for the position.
  Example: The court will likely find for the plaintiff because…
- May: Maybe. This should be used if there is not strong support for the position, but you think it is more likely than not.
  Example: The court may find for the plaintiff because…
- May not: This is the converse of may and should likewise be used when the support is weak.
  Example: The court may not find for the plaintiff because…
- Unlikely: This is the converse of likely and should likewise be used when there is strong support.
  Example: The court is unlikely to find for the plaintiff because…
- Will not: This is the converse of Will and should be used just as sparingly.
  Example: The court will not find for the plaintiff because…

It is important to fully explain your analysis. This is where the fun lawyering skills come into play, and will be an important skill for you in practice. In order to maximize your score, remember to explain every inference you make within your analysis. Here are a few examples related to federal subject matter jurisdiction with respect to diversity jurisdiction. Do not worry if you have not covered this topic yet in civil procedure, all you need to know for this specific example to make sense is there is currently a statutory requirement of damages above $75,000.

> *Good*: The amount in controversy is likely met because there are medical bills.

This is a good response because you have been able to identify the key fact in the fact pattern that gives rise to the inference the amount in controversy has been established.

> *Better*: The amount in controversy is likely met because there are medical bills for the six months of recovery.

This is a better response because you have provided more detail to support the inference that the medical bills satisfy the amount in controversy.

> *Best*: The amount in controversy is likely met because the medical bills for six months of recovery are customarily above $75,000.

This is the best response because you have provided sufficient detail to support the inference that medical bills satisfy the amount in controversy by drawing upon your general knowledge of the real world and articulating an inference you have made about the medical bills in relation to the amount in controversy.

To develop your legal writing skills, try to omit ambiguous words. Clearly state each party and omit words like "it" in favor of explaining the concept. You want your reader to follow your analysis, and you do not want to confuse parties as you are writing.

Counter Arguments and Defenses (Not to Be Confused with Affirmative Defenses)

As part of your analysis, you should include any applicable counter arguments and defenses. In the amount in controversy above,

> Example: The defendant may assert there is no liability for trespass since the defendant did not know he was walking across the plaintiff's property to pick the flower; however, this argument is unlikely to succeed because the intent required in trespass is willful conduct not knowledge of boundary lines.

This example explains a potential counter argument, but discredits the persuasiveness of the argument by asserting the applicable legal standard. The example is a single sentence, albeit a long one. If the matter is more complex, then you may need to devote a little more time to the analysis in the essay. Remember, you are under a time constraint so the goal is to identify counter arguments, discredit them, and move on quickly.

Privileges and Affirmative Defenses

You may want to think of affirmative defenses and privileges in this context: yes, all of those elements are satisfied, but it does not matter. Now you might be thinking, wait a minute, the poor plaintiff just established their case! Here is an example of an affirmative defense in action:

> While the plaintiff can likely establish a prima facia case of battery, the defendant will likely prevail by asserting self defense because the plaintiff punched the plaintiff first.

Then you will go on to explain the rule for self defense and the explanation just as we walked through above. You guessed it, here is another CRAC in your essay. We started with a conclusory statement, will go on to provide the rule and explain how to apply the rule, and then use the facts to analyze the claim.

Privileges are similar. Here is a basic example: A paramedic responding to an emergency enters the property to aid an ailing homeowner. While all of the elements for trespass may be met, in this case the privilege will excuse the paramedic from liability for trespass. And that makes sense, right? We want first responders to be able to respond to emergencies. This is an example of public policy. Public policy supports excluding paramedics from liability for trespass when a paramedic responded to an emergency of an ailing homeowner.

Conclusion

Ending with a conclusion of your analysis is the final step in CRAC and IRAC. We get it, if you started with a conclusory statement, it can feel a little repetitive to end with the same idea. It is an expected part of legal form and it may help to think of this as your final move. You can also use this as an opportunity to weave in public policy as mentioned above. Your conclusion closes the issue with a stance on the issue analyzed. Nothing is worse than an essay that ends with, "who knows"? Pick a side, hopefully the stronger side, and drive it home.

7.2 Additional Tips & Tricks

When the Fact Pattern Is not Clear on a Particular Point

Sometimes there is ambiguity in a fact pattern. Sometimes this is intentional by your professor, sometimes extensive fact patterns leave a particular point out. If you come across this scenario, do not panic. Skim through the fact pattern again to make sure you did not overlook the needed bit of information. After you have confirmed the information is not included the best way to handle this is by addressing it straight on. Here is a simplified example:

> The fact pattern does not indicate whether or not the plaintiff apprehended the defendant's conduct. If the plaintiff apprehended the

> defendant's contact, the plaintiff will likely prevail on a claim of assault. If the plaintiff was unaware of the defendant's punch and simply luckily moved out of the path by chance unaware of the impending contact, it is unlikely the plaintiff will prevail on a claim for assault.

In this example, we analyzed both potential outcomes of the claim. We started with identifying the missing information and then supplying the possible outcomes. Next, we will infer which scenario is more likely so we can keep moving through our analysis:

> It is likely the plaintiff was aware of the defendant's impending punch and dodged out of the way as dodging a punch by chance is a rare occurrence.

When this type of ambiguity arises, the legal issue is typically a little more complex. In any event, using this approach, you will be prepared to handle it like a pro.

Next Steps

At this point you have gotten through your first issue, but remember how we made that whole list of issues? You need to do this process for each issue. Sometimes professors are agreeable to shortcuts, meaning you can reference previous analysis in the next issue to cut down on redundancy, but other professors may want it spelled out each time. This means that your essay is going to have numerous CRACs, one for each issue. Occasionally you may be presented with a fact pattern wherein there is only one issue to discuss; sign us up for that class because it is a rare treat in law school!

Notably, minor issues may have a CRAC that is very brief, and may even omit some parts. In that list of issues you made, you noted causes of action that were not applicable. Here is a super short example of an CRAC:

> Battery is inapplicable because there was no contact or even indirect contact, only fear of imminent contact. As contact is an element of battery, plaintiff will not be able to establish a prima facia case of battery because plaintiff easily dodged the defendant's punch and did not experience any contact as a result of moving away from the imminent contact. Thus the defendant will not be found liable for this cause of action.

With the method outlined above, you have gotten the crux of the available points. Now to add icing to the cake, because that is our style. If time permits, you will want to add a conclusion to both the beginning and the end of the essay. The beginning conclusion should act as a road map, providing your predicted outcome for each issue. The ending conclusion should reinforce each of the issues analyzed.

Here is an example of each:

> *Beginning Road Map Conclusory Statement*: While the plaintiff is likely to establish contract formation by the parties oral agreement, the agreement is unlikely to be enforceable as the Statute of Frauds requires property purchases to be reduced to writing. However, the plaintiff will likely prevail on a theory of estoppel because the plaintiff moved onto the property and made substantial improvements.

> *Ending Conclusion*: Beginning as analyzed, the plaintiff is likely to establish contract formation by the parties oral agreement; however, the agreement is unlikely to be enforceable as the Statute of Frauds requires property purchases to be reduced to writing. As the plaintiff moved onto the property with the defendant's consent and made substantial improvements to the property with the defendant's knowledge, the plaintiff is likely to prevail under a theory of estoppel.

7.3 Homestretch

Organization matters. Your professors do not want a big, jumbled mess. Remember how we started with the alphabet soup? Now that you have gotten through the components of the essay, you may want to circle back one more time to the beginning.

A note of caution: Some professors are sticklers for form. This means that a standalone sentence on a rule from a case illustration does not belong in the middle of your analysis section. These professors would prefer the case analogy to the current fact pattern be contained in a single sentence. You will likely encounter this particularity more in the context of memo and brief writing, but a note of caution is in order as you do not want to lose points for putting your sentences in the wrong order on an exam essay. And yes, law school can be that competitive. Remember, everyone in law school is smart and it is often seemingly minutiae that separates grades.

JESSICA'S TIP — x

If you aren't sure how the analysis should be structured for a given topic, ask your professor. It's important that you understand not only the concepts, but how to structure the concepts within an analysis.

As a rule of thumb, there are going to be some anchor concepts that are more likely to be in an essay and there are some rules that lend themselves better to testing via multiple choice questions. If you are in contracts, there is a great likelihood that you will be writing about contract formation in an essay. As you are preparing for essay writing, try to think about the concepts that are most likely to be tested in an essay format. If you are not certain, using commercial products will likely help you uncover consistent topics from your course that are coming up in model essays. This may not perfectly align with your professor's exam model, but it is a great step in the right direction towards building your base knowledge.

SARAH'S STORY — x

My essay writing skills at the start of first semester were subpar. It's a skill that I really focused on developing. Using the formulated approach of CRAC was really difficult for me, but once I got the hang of it, my essays improved dramatically. I usually copy and paste my rule after writing it. The second version of my rule becomes the anchor for my analysis section so I remember to step through each element discretely. I also learned to use the word "because" and explain my inferences—can't stress that enough!

Your professor may be willing to provide model essay responses or sample student essay responses. Sometimes these are available on the school website, so it is great to check there. If your professor does not have any samples on the website, but another professor teaching your course does, it does not hurt to look through those essays. It may not be the particular format your professor prefers, but it gives you a good idea of the topics that are routinely tested in an essay format for the course. If your professor does not have any samples on the website, it never hurts to ask for some!

If you are able to track down some sample essays, it is important to know whether it is a model answer or a student answer. A model answer covers all the things your professor was looking for in an exam response, whereas a student essay provides a solid starting point but it may have missed addressing an issue or have gone down a tangent. Often essays are written to cover more topics than the time constraints allow; if the model essay looks insurmountable, know that it may not have been written in the same time constraints you will be facing. Likewise, try not to be too hard on a student essay, as this is one of the top grades and shows you what the professor is looking for from students.

As you are reading a model or student answer, try to first look at the format used—IRAC, CRAC, etc. Then look at the rule statement formulation and note any differences in rules from your own practice essay. You may find a better way of phrasing something, or that you have learned a rule this semester from a new case that was not around when the model or student answer was drafted. Additionally, take note of whether the model or student essay includes case names and how they have organized the content. This will give you great insights on how you should plan to approach your organization and inclusion of cases. Additionally, take note of the portion of time spent on each issue in relation to the fact pattern and the order of the issues discussed. This will help you understand how to order your issues in a similar fact pattern and the amount of time to dedicate to each.

Let us step back for a moment. If you are practicing essay writing and have difficulty with the time constraints, you may need to practice typing. This is a basic skill, but it will make or break you on a timed exam and it is a skill you can improve upon. Most professors do not mark down a significant amount for misspelled words. If typing is tough and spell check is not included, you may need to accept a little less accuracy in favor of having time to demonstrate your knowledge. This is one of the few times where quantity is more important than quality. If pressed for time, leave the misspelled words and keep typing. If you continue experiencing difficulties with your timed essays, you may need to revisit the accommodations process discussed in Chapter 5.

BETHANY'S TIP — X

Each writing class you take will be slightly different, but the basic concepts will remain the same. Maintaining access to your previous submissions to remind yourself of how a certain technique is structured is a great reason to keep your documents updated. Also, be sure to go back and revise your materials based on feedback, even if it does not count toward your grade. These can be used for writing samples later, and the last thing you will want to do is miss a deadline for an internship or job application because you cannot find the feedback from your first semester.

Key Takeaways

- Use a formal writing style for your essay response.
- Work through each issue in the order of importance.
- Identify the key legal issue and applicable rules, apply the facts, and state your conclusion.
- Practice your typing. Seriously.

▷▷▷ 8

The Mad Dash to Midterms

It is right before midterms and you may be in a panic. Take a deep breath and relax. Your first midterm is one grade, and ultimately may have very little impact on your overall grade. We are not saying do not give it your best effort, but do not get so focused on the grade that you let everything else slide because you cannot turn it around, or you are clearly set and do not need to worry about studying.

Did you hear your classmate did 150 practice questions while you only fit in time for 5 plus an essay? Did another person bring up a case that was in the supplement while you only focused on assigned cases? Oh well! The point is that you should show up as your best self, as prepared as you can be to take the test. If your best is only 5 questions, that is OK. Make a goal to fit in 10 questions next time. It can be helpful to know other's study efforts and to learn new techniques or habits, but in the end, you are the only one who can make a plan that best works for you. Some people inflate their numbers, some people take longer to study, and others may simply just have more time to use for studying. Do not allow mental comparison to be a barrier to your success.

Depending on the outcome, this may be the first time that you have ever seen a grade so low. You are now in the land of folks who care about their academic success. Think back to your high school experience—there were definitely folks who cared about their grades and others who had different goals. In law school, imagine you are up against a bunch of you. We promise it is not the end of the world if you did not get the A, and in the end, C's still get degrees.

8.1 Professor Expectations

How do you know what your professor is looking for and will be testing on the exam? Most likely they have told you either directly or indirectly.

Sometimes professors will comment that "this is important," "if this is on the exam," or "people often get this wrong on the exam." Hopefully you make a note of this when you are taking notes during class. Star it or highlight it when you hear these comments during class. The professors are being nice enough to give you a direct warning, so these are mistakes you should be able to avoid. It also is a hint of what the professor expects.

For example, if a Constitutional Law professor says, "If you are analyzing the Necessary and Proper clause, you must be analyzing some other legislative power as well," there is no reason that you should ever analyze the Necessary and Proper Clause without bringing in another topic such as the Commerce Clause. If a professor is nice enough to tell you what the common mistakes are, take note so you can avoid them.

Another helpful piece of information is what format does your professor want your essay in: IRAC or CRAC? Believe it or not, phrasing that first sentence as an issue question or a conclusion can make a significant difference in the scoring simply because of the preference of some professors.

Regardless of which method your professor prefers, make sure you have a conclusion. If you are writing sequentially on a timed test, your end conclusion will be lost if you run out of time. CRAC avoids this issue because you have already stated your conclusion once. If the professor prefers IRAC, write your conclusion statement first.

Some professors in specific classes adhere to the CRAP method. CRAP covers: (1) Conclusion, (2) Rule Statement, (3) Analysis, and (4) Policy Consideration. Even if your professor does not mention a need to include the policy considerations in the essay, if your class spends a lot of time focusing on policy considerations and you have time, include them.

In order to get a better feel for the professor's expectations, you can always check with your professor or the library to see if they have old practice exams you can look at. These help you understand how the professor words questions, as well as how they score. A model answer can show what the professor was looking for, as well as how the points were broken out per topic. After seeing how the professor breaks down the scoring for a topic, you can tell the level of emphasis on different areas (rules in general, specific elements, case names, etc.) and guess which parts will gain you more points within the question.

Check with your professor to know if they expect case names within an exam essay. Some classes require case names, while for others it may be a professor preference. It is possible that as long as you know the fact pattern and holding in order to compare or contrast within the analysis of the essay, you will be fine.

Knowing cases and current events can help when preparing for the exam because often the exam question will be analogous to a case or two that the class covered. When a news story relates to a similar topic and can be used to create a unique hypothetical twist, you may just see that fact pattern on your exam.

8.2 Grades and the Curve

JESSICA'S STORY — x

In undergrad, my school was notorious for grade deflation. While there were always stories about universities using grade inflation, my classmates and I knew that we were fighting the opposite battle, with professors intentionally giving lower grades in what I can only imagine was an attempt to make the university appear to have a tougher program. Even grade deflation did not prepare me for law school grading.

Professors seem to grade one of two ways: everyone scores really well, or everyone scores really poorly. The poor raw scores can be done with what seems like tough grading, or it can be done by having an impossible number of points available to score (think over 1,000 points, but the highest score is only in the 400s).

Regardless of how the professor grades, ultimately a professor will be putting your grade on a curve. The exact curve varies, but generally can be found on the school website or through a quick internet search. The curve varies based on which "year" you are in, but if your program is part time and extended over more than three years, you will not be getting that upperclassmen curve until the university has determined you have reached the equivalent completed credits of a 2L. That can take three to four semesters depending on the program.

When looking at grades prior to the final grade, do not assume the percentages correspond with the letter grade that you have been accustomed to throughout your education. We have been told quite bluntly by professors and deans that "90% doesn't mean A work." This is a bitter pill to swallow for most people, and tends to make for an excessively competitive environment.

When your grades come out, there are two things to consider: (1) what percentage of my total grade is this; and (2) how does my score compare to the average score and the score range. These two factors are crucial to give you perspective on how you did, and may inspire you to pursue accommodations if you have not previously. (Revisit Chapter 5 if you happened to skip that section the first time around.)

The percentage of your grade is a key fact to know. Traditionally, the final exam was the only assessment, meaning there was no opportunity to truly see what the professor likes and get feedback. Many professors have now broken that up more, and will have at least a midterm, if not a combination of midterm, quizzes, other assignments, and participation. In almost every class the final is at least 50% of the total grade, and can be 70% or more. That means that your score right now, no matter how good or bad, can shift dramatically at final exam time. This is important to remember. Do not let a seemingly low score get you so down and distracted that you do not perform as well as you should on later assessments and the final. It is really easy to overcome the fact that you only got 5 points on a 10 point exam worth only 10% of the grade. At the same time, if you do really well (congratulations!), do not coast until finals. That final grade is still anyone's game.

Comparing scores can be one of the most useful tools you have when considering your grade. Most of the time the professor will give you an average grade and a range, and if they do not, ask for it. You can tell a lot about how you compare to your class on any given assessment based on where you are in relation to the average. The other important factor is the range. If the scores range from 35% to 100%, it can be really upsetting if you have a 50. If the class average with a range of 35% to 100% is 50, you can say with relative certainty that most of the scores are on the low end, whereas if the average is 85, you know the majority of the class got high scores. This gives you an idea if the score on the high or the low end may actually just be an outlier that is representative of the class or if there really is a dramatic spread. This information can give you a rough comparison of where you are compared to your class, and you can guess if your 50% would potentially be a C or C+ if the final did not exist or was more likely a D. If you have multiple assessments covering different areas, you can see how you compare to other students in each area and where you need to focus more energy to be competitive when final exam time comes.

A key aspect of law school grading is that the professor cannot really tell you what letter grade you are currently at because so much of your grade has not been evaluated, and the grades will not be figured out until the very end. There is no progress report part way through the semester beyond those ranges and comparing your total points to the range of your classmates on each exam. Some professors may update you on the class range overall periodically, but others will not and you can only assume that the person who got the top and bottom score each time was the same. Adding up the average points per each score, out of the total points up to that point, and comparing your score is not an exact indication of where you are, but can help if you are nervous.

For proof that your midterm grade does not define your final grade, here are one of the author's grades for different classes at midterms versus the final grade:

Class	**At Midterms**	**Final Grade**
Torts 1	Just below average	A+ (highest in class)
Property 1	Average	A (highest in class)
Civil Procedure 1	Just above average	A+
Civil Procedure 2	At the bottom of the upper quartile	A-
Contracts 1	Below average/bottom quartile	A
Constitutional Law 1	Below average/bottom quartile	B+

8.3 Quiet Period

Whether your school calls it something other than a quiet period or not, many law schools have a certain period of time after taking an exam where students are prohibited from discussing the contents of the exam with anyone (except a designated person like the registrar to report technical errors). This means students cannot speak with each other about the exam and they are unable to reach out to professors during this time period. It is always best practice to confirm the quiet period has ended before engaging your peers or professors.

It is so tempting after an exam to reach out to your law school friends to commiserate together. They say misery loves company, right? But an honor code violation probably is not on your bucket list. Also, your energy is better spent preparing for your next exam, paper, weekly reading, or whatever is on your to-do list. This may sound harsh but it is not. The practice of law is going to be the same way. You will deal with something really challenging and then need to put it on the back burner for a hot second and attend to your next client.

The emotions you are feeling are real and you may need an outlet to rant about it. Hang in there, the quiet period will be over before you know it. You may find you have a little healthier perspective once the quiet period ends and your rant will likely be less fueled by emotion and shift towards a more logical analysis of the exam experience. You and your friends will end up spending less energy rehashing the negatives and more time learning to shift to the next task and engaging in analysis together. You will likely identify study gaps and areas of weakness to shore up. Take the time to review, but try not to wallow. You may even come to enjoy the emotional guardrail that the quiet period provides.

BETHANY'S STORY — x

Are you looking at those grades and starting to tremble a bit? I promise you, those are not what my grades look like. I didn't get my first "A" in law school until well into year two. There were times where I was at the top of the curve or even right at the curve until the final, and dropped substantially. It was hard. I came from an academic background where A's were the norm for me, so when I hit my first semester with a B+ in every course, I was devastated. I even had to take a GRASP class at some point in my career. (AKA, I scored a flat C or lower in a doctrinal class.)

But, look: here I am still with the chance to write this book, as well as work full-time, and experience all of the great things I am filling my resume with along the way. There's a proverbial saying that your grades correlate with your future: A's in law school become professors, B's lawyers, and C's judges. I don't know the data on if that's actually true or not, but my goal is to do my best, stay in academic good standing, and pass the bar. So far, so good.

Also, me saying that I'm OK with my grades where they are was a journey. Ask my husband: there were tears. There were times when I thought my future career in law was lost. If you're struggling with your grades, either externally or internally, set a meeting up with your success coach. I meet with my success coach regularly, even in the good semesters, to ensure I am staying on track and reviewing any habits that might not be serving me well. Find your success coach and check in often!

8.4 Burnout

Burnout is a scary word, and is equally as scary to experience. Burnout happens when one is overly exhausted, be it emotionally, physically, or otherwise, due to prolonged stress exposure. This can be brought on by not only law school in general, but add to it the stressors of being online and dealing with technology issues, other responsibilities at home, job expectations, and also increased pressure from midterms or the curve. It is important to take a moment to pause and reflect on your stress levels and how to mitigate them when they are becoming overwhelming.

Counseling can be a great avenue. If you already have a counselor you connect with regularly, great. Also, many universities provide some level of counseling to students. Be sure to double check that if you attend a program that is located in another state, that the counseling services are still able to extend to you. If not, you can always ask for a referral for a more local option—or even an online option in your state.

Take time to unplug. There will be times where it feels as though you can never get away from your monitor due to the mountain of work you need to complete for school. That is one of the best times to get up and away and do something completely unrelated to the program. Whether it is a night away, or just 20 minutes, allowing your brain to reset can make such a difference in your mindset for your work.

Try to figure out what works best for you before you reach this stage so you have a plan to put into place. Know that you are not alone and that you can get through this.

Key Takeaways

- Know your professor's expectations heading into the midterm.
- Midterms are important, but final grades are still anyone's game.
- Evaluate your performance and identify which areas you need to work on prior to finals.
- Always confirm when the quiet period has ended before engaging peers or professors.

▷▷▷ 9

Inside Scoop on Legal Writing

Legal writing courses cover memo and brief writing in depth. This chapter is not intended to supplant your legal writing classes, since it is a high level overview of memos and briefs, ending with the differences from exam essay writing. Enjoy this inside scoop on legal writing—you may find it pairs well with a bowl of ice cream. Many things in law school pair well with a bowl of your favorite treat!

A memo is generally written objectively and evaluates the strength of a legal issue. There are many applications for memos, from judicial bench memos to writing a memo as your final. Attorneys routinely write memos to clients and memos to the client's file as a record. That is right, memos are a staple pantry item of legal writing. Here is an objectively written assertion:

> The Defendant was driving 56 mile per hour on a street that had a speed limit of 35 miles per hour.

Likewise, briefs permeate the industry. However, unlike memos, briefs are usually written persuasively. Briefs are most commonly filed with the court; however, briefs are used in arbitration settings as well. Many jurisdictions limit the number of pages of a brief and have very specific filing requirements, such as font size and margins. An important thing to remember with brief writing is that you are advocating for a side. This means that you are writing it in favor of your client. Here is a persuasively written assertion:

> The Defendant was driving excessively fast, over 20 miles per hour above the speed limit, and thereby endangering lives.

Both of these examples covered assertions that are made within the analysis segment of a brief or memo. However, the objectiveness or persuasiveness is used throughout. From the statement of facts to the framing of your rules, every segment of your memo is completely objective and every segment of your brief is persuasively written to benefit your client.

When writing a brief, using a theme can help your reader connect to your content. It is a commonality that is subtly repeated throughout your writing to help your reader (i.e., the judge or your professor) understand why your client's side should prevail. If you need a concrete example of a theme, take a quick moment and Google "if the glove doesn't fit you must acquit." This was a trial theme, but it translates to persuasive writing as well.

You will likely see this paralleled in your law school experience with brief and memo assignments having very clearly defined requirements for fonts, margins, spacing, page limitations, etc. It is important to follow these criteria precisely, just as you will need to in practice someday. In fact, many jurisdictions have moved to online filing so you will be well-prepared for this component of practice.

A good issue statement uses an "Under, Does, When" method and is usually the starting point for both memos and briefs. This is the roadmap that lays forth the legal analysis to follow. Here is how it works:

> Under (insert law), does (insert alleged legal issue), when (insert supporting/opposing facts).

It looks pretty simple, but crafting this sentence is an art form. It requires you to drill down and really understand the applicable law, the issue, and the facts that either support or are in contrast to the legal issue. Your professor is likely to read every single word of your brief or memo; however, a busy judge may not have as much time. Learning to write this sentence well tees up the rest of your legal writing and helps your reader get straight to the most important content.

Judges and attorneys are busy people, so always put your strongest arguments first and then continue through the rest. It can feel like you need to finish with a big bang, but that is not how legal writing is done and a judge is not going to think that you think it is a strong argument if it is placed last. Let your conclusion be your shining wrap-up.

A key difference between memos and briefs as compared to essay writing on a final exam is the inclusion of references. References in memos and briefs follow The Bluebook or other designated source. In a law school essay exam, typically professors have students reference a case by name, whereas a memo or brief will require the reporter, pincite, court, year, etc. The Bluebook citations can feel like a lot to learn, but you will get the hang of it with practice if it is not naturally apparent to you. If you are struggling with citations, librarians are a great source, but be mindful of any honor code limitations associated with your class.

Related to case citations is legal research. In order to cite the cases, you will first need to find them! We covered legal research in Chapter 4 so feel free to circle back if you need a refresher. Again, your librarians are master researchers and can generally find anything. There may be limitations on using librarian support for your assignments though, so make sure you fully understand this piece before reaching out for help.

You will want to take some time prior to submitting your paper to check through all of your citations to make sure there have not been any case holding changes. This will be the same process you will use in practice prior to submitting your filing to the court. This is a key step to avoiding malpractice, so to reiterate, always verify that your citations are still good law. Always.

Additionally, you need to use a full CREXAC or CREAC method (as designated by your professor) for memo and brief writing as opposed to an essay. We covered the alphabet soup in Chapter 7 if you need to review these acronyms. Your case illustrations will generally be much more robust. And that makes sense because essay writing in an exam is done under strict time constraints (usually 30 to 60 minutes) whereas memos and briefs are usually drafted under longer periods of time.

Editing is significantly different for memos and briefs than on exam essays. On an exam essay, you may have a couple of typos and missed commas. In writing a legal brief or memo, you will spend a significant amount of time perfecting your writing. Legal professionals tend to expect perfection and will harshly judge obvious errors. From formatting your citations to crafting a perfect opening sentence, your approach to writing matters. You will want to print out a paper copy of your writing because it can be easier to spot things on paper than electronic format. You will also want to read the pages out of order. When you become so familiar with your writing, it can be difficult to catch errors because you know what you meant to say even if it's not quite what you actually wrote. Your essay during an exam may have very little editing in stark contrast to the hours you will spend editing your brief or memo.

SARAH'S STORY — x

I always use the "Read Aloud" feature in Microsoft Word. It is painful to go through every single word, sentence, paragraph, and page, but it's one of the best way for me to catch mistakes.

Lastly, in case you have not picked up on this theme yet, attorneys and judges are pressed for time. Some students struggle with the page limitations imposed. It may sound crazy, because for other students filling eighteen pages (or whatever your assignment allotted) may sound like an impossible feat. A key skill to master while you are in law school is making succinct legal arguments. You will be much better prepared in practice to master the discipline now.

SARAH'S STORY — x

Unless prohibited by your assignment, after you've completed your first draft memo or brief, conduct another quick round of legal research. Once you've wrestled through the content, you have a much firmer understanding of the case law and legal issue. You may identify a gap and fill it in with a supporting case with the second round or you can be confident in knowing you found every case you needed.

BETHANY'S STORY — x

Do not procrastinate on these assignments. Even if you were the best writer in your entire college, this is a new way of writing. Spend time rewriting phrases and editing. Play around with different techniques. Allow yourself extra time to do some last minute research to fill in the gaps. The last thing you want is to lose points for not completing an area of your memo or brief due to not allotting yourself enough buffer time.

Key Takeaways

- Memos are written objectively.
- Briefs are written persuasively.
- Put the most important things first—legal professionals are busy and always pressed for time.

▷▷▷ 10

The Importance of Taking Care of You

The legal field is not known for its priority on personal care; not many fields are. The change starts with you.

This all goes back to Maslow's hierarchy of needs.[1] At the top of the pyramid is what one can achieve if all of the other needs are met.[2] This self-actualization stage is where creation and achieving potential can happen, i.e., law school.[3] Going backwards down the pyramid, it includes psychological and basic needs. One cannot self-actualize if they do not feel connected and confident.[4] One cannot create those connections if they do not feel safe nor have basic living needs met.[5]

In law school, you will be pushed to exist in the self-actualization stage at all times. However, that is not realistic. You will have moments, days, and sometimes even weeks where you will not be able to prioritize academic work. There is a lie that exists that success is all about finding balance. News flash: there is no perfect balance. It is about doing your best to plan and having a backup plan when life happens.

---

1. Abraham H. Maslow, *A theory of human motivation*, Psychological Review 50 (4): 370–396 (1943).
2. *Id.*
3. *Id.*
4. *Id.*
5. *Id.*

10.1 Find Ways to Celebrate Your Successes

Food or alcohol can be a reward, but these can also be slippery slopes to other concerns. Other rewards can be purchasing something fun and completely unnecessary for your office set-up, or even working from a vacation spot during your next week of classes. Think creatively and find ways that truly help you feel as though you have earned it, because you have.

10.2 Plan Your Connections

Whether an introvert or an extrovert, you need to spend time with other people at some point. Notice, we did not say it had to be in person, although, at some point, we do encourage you to turn off the screen. Schedule dedicated time to vent, to laugh, to complain, to discuss, or literally anything else with other people. Zoom sessions can be just as therapeutic as having someone physically sitting next to you. This is not automatically built into your schedule in an online program, and those you keep close to you in person may not understand this new, busy schedule you have. Make the time, and honor it.

10.3 Be OK Saying "No" or "Not Today"

There will be times that others have expectations of you that you just do not have time for. You are the keeper of your time and well-being. Become a master at saying "no" by using creative ways of pushing it off to another day. It is hard for folks to hear you might not make it to the annual tailgate, but they will understand this expensive degree requires projects, readings, and tests that require a bit more time than you have needed to give in the past. Sometimes you just need time to sleep. No matter what the need for the "no" is, you have every right to use it.

10.4 Schedule Your Basic Needs

Sleep, hygiene, food, hair appointment … Whatever you need to be able to function, ensure it is on your calendar. No one else but you can determine what fits in this category. (Well, almost no one. Science does tell us there is a bottom line of absolute necessaries, but you get the point.) Honestly, there is no better skill you learn in law school than that of the power nap. A twenty minute snooze during your lunch break can make all the difference in surviving your next cold call.

10.5 Build in a Buffer

You likely need to arrange your schedule to build in a buffer so that unexpected things do not completely derail you. Emergencies can come up at any time and your law school may grant extensions for certain circumstances, however, life's curveballs that do not quite rise to the level of an emergency are likely to occur and you need a plan. If your tire is flat, your kiddo has a science project due tomorrow (one of those solar systems with hand painted planets), or you get a cold, having constructed your schedule with a bit of a buffer can make the world of difference. You are probably dreading this next sentence part, do not procrastinate.

10.6 Force Yourself to Do Something Non-Law-Related that Makes You Happy

OK, so maybe this one is not a direct correlation to Maslow's pyramid, but if we remade one for law school, we would include it. There will be days where you are facing a mountain of homework, have upcoming tests, and still need to complete that two hundred page reading assignment. Set yourself a timer to leave all of it in the space you have created, physically and mentally, and do something else. Do not force yourself to go clean the house, mow the grass, or respond to emails. (Although those are all great procrastination techniques, we are looking for something a tad different here.) Take anywhere from 30 minutes to a full day to go do something fun that breaks the monotony of your day-to-day schedule. Maybe a trip to a theme park with your family, a random 3:00 PM date night with your significant other, or picking up a new hobby from the overly priced craft store down the street. This kind of fun break can be exactly what your brain needs to get over the hump of feeling overwhelmed. The work will still be there, but you will be in a much better place to return to it.

10.7 Family Life Balance

By this point in your educational journey, your family may be feeling a bit neglected. This can be exacerbated if you have a spouse and kiddos in the mix as well. You may find it works well to dedicate some time each day or each week to your family relationships. Whether that is coffee with your favorite aunt, date night with your hubby, or game night with your kiddos, it is important to be intentional about consistently pouring into these relationships. Pro tip, the dedicated non-law related activity to make you happy can coincide with your family life balance needs. It can be a two-for-one type of deal!

BETHANY'S STORY — x

My husband is a lawyer and graduated from a residential program approximately five years prior to me beginning my legal journey. He has confirmed on multiple occasions how different our experiences have been. I am thankful that he is understanding that law takes a lot of energy, but knowing how different this is from even a traditional residential program has opened both our eyes. My advice is to spend time explaining what the program requires of you to your spouse ahead of time. This can save you a lot of future heartache when you have to give up so much of your time to this new element of your life.

10.8 Be OK with Shifting Responsibilities

Everyone comes to law school with a different dynamic. If you have a spouse or children, it might help you have more time to study or even spend with them if they take on a couple of more house chores while you are in law school. You might end up with a shrunken sweater or some janky mowing lines, but your whole family will be happier. The key is to figure out which things you can delegate that will not drive you bonkers and reallocate that time for studying or family time. If you have roommates or live alone, you may find some adjustments are needed there as well. Whatever your dynamic, communicating your needs with those around you can greatly help with reducing your burden for non-law school related tasks.

Key Takeaways

- You have to take care of yourself during this journey.
- Managing your time is key to your success.
- Take time for personal enjoyment each week and you will be in a much better state of mind to continue learning.

▷▷▷ 11

Involvement Outside of the Classroom

Just because you are in an online program does not mean you are precluded from on getting involved. Academically, extracurricular, and otherwise, there are plenty of options to supplement your learning either digitally or local to your area.

11.1 SBA Leadership

You will hear "SBA" thrown around a lot within the law school community. Despite being considered a "student organization," it is really a student government, similar to a high school's student council. Generally every class has representation and there is an executive board.

SBA facilitates activities and interaction among students. Events the SBA might host include mixers, Barrister's Ball, and class meetings. In addition to student events, the SBA is a link between student and faculty. A member of the executive board may be included in faculty meetings or have regular update meetings with the deans to keep communication open between the administration and the students. SBA can help facilitate changes in policies, such as changing the requirements for Latin honors or adjusting funding for student organizations.

Depending on the program, online students may have their initial class elections early in the fall semester, or they may be lumped into the online student group and have elections toward the middle to end of the spring semester, when elections for the following year occur.

If you are more event- or government-minded, this may be an organization you want to join. If you are unsure of election dates, reach out to someone at your school's SBA to find out more information and how to get involved.

11.2 Student Organizations

In addition to SBA leadership, there are many student organizations available to law schools. Many student organizations are already meeting online and they exist for just about any possible topic one could imagine. Educational law? Probably. Sports law? Yep. The list goes on. And if there is not one to fit your needs or interests, you can create one.

Many law schools host a student org fair to provide students an opportunity to learn about the various groups that are available. Most schools also have a list of student organizations, and you can email the group or group's president to get more information about joining. Groups cover all sorts of interest so everyone should be able to find something of interest. There are often groups aimed at minority groups such as: Women in Law and Leadership (WILL), Hispanic Law Student Association, Black Law Student Association, and Asian Law Students. Other groups target specific areas of law or political interests such as cannabis, the Second Amendment, intellectual property, immigration, and other federally barred topic areas.

Even if you do not feel you have time to be a full member, you can always watch for their events or speakers that may be of interest. Going to speakers, even though you are listening on a digital platform, still opens a learning experience for you that your classes may not cover. Additionally, you can get a sense if you like certain areas of law. These events may be on an online calendar, a weekly school event email, or even a group-specific email.

A word to the wise here: Do not just join organizations to have them on your resume. And trust us, there will be organizations that exist just to exist. Join them if they are actually willing to work with your schedule and remoteness as an online student, and if you have an active role. An active role does not necessarily mean a leadership position, but that would also be a great opportunity.

This is also a great way to meet other law students, network with lawyers currently in those fields, and build a relationship with your advisor (probably a law professor) who you might not otherwise get to meet. Make the most of these opportunities!

If you wish your law school had an organization to cover a specific interest area, you can always create it yourself. Being off campus may make it a little harder, but you can still reach out to the faculty advisor for student groups to start the process. You will likely need to get people to team up with you to indicate that the student body is interested in it, but those people can be other online students.

BETHANY'S TIPS

It has been hit or miss with existing student organizations for a variety of reasons. Here are some tips to get the most out of your memberships:

1. Make sure the organization is active before you pay your dues. By active, ensure they are actually having meetings and have a core of officers. Don't waste your money just for a resume filler.
2. Chat with the organization leaders to ensure online engagement is plausible and something they're willing to do. Online engagement doesn't mean someone just turning on their laptop screen and letting you watch a speaker or meeting. Engagement includes actual engagement. Think about what procedures need to be in place to ensure you're able to ask questions during meetings, participate in activities, and receive the freebies.
3. Take on a leadership role. The reality is that online engagement is still new, even outside of law schools. If leaders in a student organization haven't experienced online students as part of their group before, they are probably not sure of the best ways to engage with you. You know what it is like, so take the opportunity to advocate for yourself and fellow online students. I have found a "Hybrid Chair" to be a great role to help organizations understand the different class schedules of the online program, as well as serve as a conduit for messaging for the online program participants.
4. Be creative with engagement. There are going to be times where you just are unable to participate in the exact same way as residential members. Use this to your advantage! What are the ways that you can participate distantly to take the activities or projects to a new height? Perhaps you have connections with lawyers in a different state, are willing to send in physical items for the organization's bulletin board,

or can contribute research to the group's newsletter. The opportunities are endless to participate, even if you need to do so asynchronously.

SARAH'S EXPERIENCE — x

My first semester of law school there wasn't an SBA group for my preferred area of interest. I worked through the process with the law school and launched the new SBA organization the same semester. All it takes is a little grit, some work to gather peer support, and patience with the process. If you are passionate about a specific area of law jump in and make it happen!

11.3 Moot Court

Moot court is a competition that simulates an appellate court environment. The students who participate in moot court write practice briefs, and they present oral arguments in front of a judge. Some schools provide course credits for students participating in moot court. Moot court is one of the activities some employers specifically look for on applicants' resumes.

11.4 Trial Competition Team

Schools may also have a trial competition team, in which students are simulating a courtroom experience that may include opening and closing statements and questioning or cross-examining witnesses. This is often referred to as mock trial and is a great experience if you are interested in litigation.

11.5 Other ABA Competitions

The ABA hosts a variety of competitions for law students. To find out about the competitions watch for emails from the ABA, the law school, or notices from your professors. In order to compete in the competitions, students have to upgrade to a premium membership for a small fee (currently $25 as of 2022). Competitions can cover a variety of subjects including negotiation and interviewing/counseling.

Not only are these good resume builders, but the events are great learning experiences. You can see other teams' styles as you work with them while gaining unique experiences within the fields.

Even the practices leading up to the competitions allow for a very hands-on, in-depth experience where you can repeatedly practice the skills you have been learning in law school. You may find classmates have very different approaches to a methodology, despite having the same teacher, and may find techniques you want to try out and practice. The stakes are relatively low so you can try out a different style during a competition that you may otherwise not get to use.

There are many writing competitions for law students available on the ABA's website. This is a great opportunity to research and write about a topic of interest. If you are planning to work in that practice area post-law school, then having a writing sample specific to the practice area will be great for your applications!

Additionally, if competition is not your cup of tea, you may want to volunteer to assist with coordinating the event behind the scenes. Coordinating helps you to gain experience networking on a national level, while also giving you the opportunity to hone administrative skills essential to the modern-day field of law. Even volunteering for smaller, day-of-event roles (such as timekeeping) allows you to cross paths with future colleagues in the field who may have experience with various other techniques you would not have been exposed to otherwise. You get a front-row seat to observe the competitors in action!

JESSICA'S STORY

I have been lucky enough to be on the University of Dayton's Interviewing and Counseling Competition Team and on the Negotiation Team as an alternate. Both experiences were incredible. Until you repeatedly practice the same negotiation, you don't realize how many different results are possible, or what it looks like when a negotiation goes incredibly wrong and the other side refuses to close a deal because they felt your party was too pushy.

BETHANY'S TIP

Don't let your fear of performance or commitment prevent you from participating in these opportunities. There is almost always a way to be involved to boost your resume in a unique way. For example, I did not feel as though I had enough time to commit to preparing to actually compete in the competition, but volunteered to be on the planning committee. This still allowed me to connect with others in the field, gain experience, and still have enough time to hold internships and write a book.

11.6 Dean's Fellow/Teaching Assistant

If you are passionate about inspiring the next classes of law students, then you may want to consider being a dean's fellow or teaching assistant. In some situations a professor may ask if you want to fill these roles, while others require you to apply and possibly even get professor recommendations.

Being in either of these positions is a great experience and can be very rewarding, but they can also be time consuming. As a teaching assistant, you may need to proofread or grade papers and meet with students. As a dean's fellow you will likely be meeting with groups to pass on skills and tips, whether they be academic strategies, how to deal with schedules or emotions, or understanding professor preferences. You may be creating presentations as well as hosting meetings and office hours. Either of these commitments will require at least two hours a week in order to fully perform your duties, so you will want to make sure your schedule will allow for the extra time commitment.

This is a mentoring opportunity, as well as a chance to create a network with members of the other class. Despite this, do not expect that all the new students will actively participate or that you will get many thanks. Some of the students will blame you for challenges with the school and may consider you to be school staff, even if that is not your role.

JESSICA'S STORY — x

As a dean's fellow, I remember meeting with a student thanking me after getting her grades back from her first quiz. I had warned them that their first grades may not be what they expect. I had impressed upon my group that grades, especially ones that are a small percent, would not be the end of the world and that there would be plenty of opportunity to pull up the grades.

BETHANY'S TIP — x

Although having a dean's fellow was helpful in learning basic law expectations and how to lay out a memo, it can be difficult if your dean's fellow does not necessarily have similar life constraints or experience with online learning.

11.7 Scholarship

You will likely encounter books and articles written by faculty members. Scholarship is really important in the legal field. Also, it sets apart your resume from other law students and gives you something interesting to talk about in interviews down the road.

11.8 Law Review

Law review is considered a prestigious opportunity to contribute to a journal. Future employers will make positive presumptions about students that have participated in law review. Law review is typically available to 2Ls and students can either "grade on" or "write-on." If you grade onto law review it means you were automatically granted a spot by your academic performance. If you write on it means that you entered the annual competition by submitting a writing sample per the competition guidelines and were granted a coveted space.

Once law review starts, you do not really know who graded on and who wrote-on. This means that even if you do not have the strongest academic performance, but you wrote-on, a prospective employer is still going to consider you a top student. It is always a good idea to do the write-on competition just to make sure you do not miss out on the opportunity.

Law review is also a student-led organization. This means there are leadership positions within law review that are available to you, usually in your second year as a law review student. These are premium seats with the most resume appeal post-graduation.

As far as you do on law review, it is pretty simple. You write an article for publication consideration and participate in the peer review process on articles for other authors. You will have a faculty advisor, which provides an opportunity to develop a deeper connection with that professor. You will want to choose a faculty advisor who is knowledgeable about your article topic. You can also reach out to attorneys in the industry and ask their advice—it is a great way to network!

11.9 Writing for Other Journals or Professional Organizations

Whether or not you do law review at your school, you are always able to write articles for other journals and professional organizations. This might sound daunting, but rest assured, it happens routinely. You will want to identify areas of interest, draft the article, and then send the submission to journals and professional organizations with aligned interests.

Or maybe you will get inspired and write a textbook! Whatever route(s) you take, scholarship is a great way to develop deeper knowledge of an area of law and is a huge resume booster, so it is a two-for-one type of deal.

SARAH'S TIP — x

Writing an article for a professional organization gave me the opportunity to work with two Big Law attorneys, who both specialized in a practice area of interest to me. This experience enriched my understanding and helped me build deeper connections with attorneys at two different firms.

11.10 Pro Bono

For some programs, pro bono work is built in as a requirement. For others, it is optional, yet encouraged. Either way, we would suggest you participate in it.

Pro bono opportunities are a great way to give back to your community while gaining invaluable experience. Programs tend to have a particular way to record hours and what type of work counts toward pro bono hours. Be sure to consistently check the requirements, and submit your paperwork with time to spare so that it is not a mad dash to collect everything before the deadline.

11.11 State Bar & Other Professional Associations

What better way to get to know the field than to join it?

Not only do you have your main state bar association, but there are usually smaller subsections, as well. Look for local bar associations, as well as identity-based ones.

Bar associations will not only maintain your registration to practice law, but also provide CLE development opportunities. Yes, even post-graduation there is an expectation to keep learning. Many bar associations even offer free or reduced cost memberships to students, as well as access to the CLEs. These are a great resource if you are interested in a specific area of law that will not be covered by your academic program, as well as the more logistical side of running an ethical practice.

Similarly, if you are looking for hands-on practice in a certain area, or just trying to determine which area(s) of law you are interested in, check out their volunteer opportunities. Training is usually provided, and they are always in need of more assistance. There seems to be a flux of opportunities moving to remote availability post-COVID. If they have an event that is just in-person, ask for a way to participate remotely or volunteer to help make remote participation a possibility. They are usually more than willing to find a way to make it happen. It is a great way to network and add to your resume!

SARAH'S STORY — x

One semester during 1L, my daughter had surgery shortly before finals. It was a tough semester to say the least, but through that experience, I realized our state had yet to enact legislation to protect those with disabilities from discrimination with respect to organ transplants. During winter break I got to work putting together the information I needed to drive the project forward. My mentor at our state bar recommended I reach out to my legislator.

I scheduled coffee and presented my findings, along with draft legislation drawing from other states that had taken the step to protect this vulnerable population. I was afforded the opportunity to serve on the drafting committee alongside the team of attorneys and also had the chance to spend time at our state capitol during the legislative session. It was an incredibly rewarding experience and the Governor's office reached out right away to pledge support. The bill passed the House without any opposition and it went through the Senate with flying colors. The Governor signed the bill, and our state now has this protective measure in place. The state bar is full of amazing people willing to help point you in the right direction. Law school will help shape a mindset of advocacy and enable you to take on incredible projects for the betterment of humanity.

Key Takeaways

- Participating in activities outside of the classroom is a great way to enrich your education.
- Getting involved is not one size fits all; pick the path that works for you because the opportunities are endless (well, almost endless).
- You have several years in law school, so you have plenty of time to explore different avenues of involvement.

▷▷▷ 12

Charting Your Career

12.1 Current Career

You may have a difficult time finding that balance of law school and your career. If this resonates with you, hang in there and keep reading. If you are not currently navigating this, feel free to jump down to the next section.

There is no magic here; it takes work and you may need to try a couple of different things before you find the right method. Rest assured, those that have gone before you have been successful. It is not a small undertaking and we are applauding you every step of the way. You can do it: Law school is doable.

You will likely have to make some sacrifices, like more dry shampoo and a few microwave dinners, but you can do it. Communicate with your support system and let them know what you need on the home front so that you can keep your career going and also do well in law school. You may also need to relax some of your standards and be more disciplined in your time blocks. Think about ordering your groceries or getting a house cleaner if you can afford it.

If you happen to have kiddos, it is incredible for them to see you working hard and growing professionally. The impact of you attending school will have a lasting impression and influence their lives in really beautiful ways. One of the best things you can do is to spend some intentional time with your children. Yes, you will have less time overall, so try to make sure the time you do spend together is quality time.

SARAH'S TIP — X

I have figured out that what works best for my life is to switch laundry and load the dishwasher first thing in the morning, well, right after I brush my teeth. As a mom of two daughters, keeping up with housework and finding time to be a mom/wife has been challenging. I still drive my daughter to and from school daily. While the bus may be a time saver, that's my special dedicated time with her every day.

You may find that you need to transition to part-time work, but we understand that may be cost-prohibitive or otherwise not an option for you. In any event, some jobs offer more flexibility and it is certainly worth considering if you are really struggling to balance everything.

BETHANY'S TIP — X

Being up-front with my place of employment has been key to my success. Letting them know when finals are, or that I need certain times away for classes, has been essential to ensure I am able to balance the needs of both aspects of my life. This has been a very different experience from colleagues I've worked with who were concurrently completing a PhD program. Law school is different, and not everyone understands just how different it is until they've experienced it themselves.

12.2 Preparing for Your Future Career

Law school is not just about getting a degree, but also about preparing for your career. It may be a new career altogether or expanding within your current role. Either way, remember that you are here for more than a degree.

The legal industry is a big, beautiful world. Even if you came to law school with a strong sense of what your career goals are, you might find it helpful to take a moment along the way to consider all the legal world has to offer. Either you will affirm your current direction if you have already got it mapped out, or you may find a whole new area that captures your interest.

12.3 Practice Areas

The list is endless. Any industry you can think of, they need an attorney. A quick look through a course catalog will give you a sense of the legal topics typically covered in law school. This non-exhaustive list includes Family Law, Intellectual Property, Constitutional Law, Property, Torts, Healthcare Law, Sports Law, Employment Law, Tax Law, Bankruptcy Law, Environmental Law, Securities, Educational Law, Immigration, Criminal Law, Contractual Law, etc. The required law school curriculum covers a wide range of topics, and you may have the opportunity to select elective courses in areas of particular interest to you. In addition to the practice area, there are different ways to practice law within a specific area. For example, if you are interested in practicing property law, as a transactional attorney you may be involved with drafting closing documents and performing titles searches, whereas a litigator would be involved in advocating on behalf of their client in property disputes. Here are some broad categories to think about:

- Transactional (think drafting)
  - Wills & Trusts
  - Contracts
  - Entity Formation
  - Policies
- Litigation (think writing briefs and court appearance, with most cases settling before trial)
  - Criminal Defense
  - Criminal Prosecution
  - Plaintiff's Attorney
  - Civil Defense Attorney
- Mediation/Arbitration
- Legal Adjacent

12.4 Practice Settings

Beyond the type of law you are interested in, there are many different settings in which to practice. Here is a broad list of settings to consider along the way:

- Public Service: City, County, State, or Federal
- Law Firm: Big Law, Mid-Sized, Small, or Solo
- In-House Counsel: Start-Up to Fortune 500
- Public Interest Groups and Nonprofits
- Academia

Having an understanding of the legal landscape will help you think about the type of setting or settings that you may enjoy working in. Moreover, you can start strategizing to gain experiences to become a stronger candidate for your end goals. It is also OK if you have no clue what area of practice or type of setting you might like to work in. The great news about law school is that you will have plenty of time to figure that out along the way, and possibly even change your mind a few times.

12.5 Nuts & Bolts

Career services is a great place to get started, whether you are seeking information on internships or starting to network for post-graduation goals. Career services can help you understand the employment landscape and connect you with alumni working in areas of interest to you. In a few short years, you will likely be in that database and have the chance to help a law student!

Typically internship employers request a resume, unofficial transcript, writing sample, and cover letter. You may find internship opportunities at any time, whether it is through a school career services email, LinkedIn, or local bar association newsletter, but they often have very close deadlines. It is a good idea to keep these documents at your fingertips, already compiled, so it is quicker and easier to apply without adding another thing to your never-ending to-do list.

First things first, your resume. There are a couple of different ways to format your resume. Some entities prefer more old-school, vanilla-style resumes and other firms will be open to having a more modern style that reflects your personality. You will probably find that you need to have a version of each. Government, Big Law, and larger corporations tend to prefer the more traditional style of resume. Start-ups and nonprofits seem more open to modern style resumes. Do a little research before sending in your resume to determine which style the entity may be most open to receiving.

As to the rest of your materials, for your unofficial transcripts, simply print to PDF an unofficial transcript at the end of each semester. Also, you can have a baseline cover letter drafted and just modify it for the particular opportunity—this is a huge time saver instead of drafting from scratch each time. For your writing sample, as you progress through law school you'll want your writing sample to reflect more complex legal concepts to get a leg up on the competition. Writing samples are typically 4–10 pages and include a segment from a brief or memo. It's important to provide an introductory paragraph so that your reader has an understanding of the material being presented and is not randomly dropped into the legal issue. Make sure you know any page requirements and proofread your writing sample meticulously, since you want to start with your best foot forward.

Naturally, interviewing follows your application. OCI stands for On Campus Interview. Some law schools offer OCI opportunities for top tier students to interview with firms that typically hire graduates from the law school. If you are lucky enough to snag one of these spots, make the most of it because an OCI is an incredible opportunity. OCI interviews are great for landing summer internships and also for post-graduation roles.

The pioneer route is the next option. If you are not offered OCI, whether by academic performance, geography, or some other reason, do not fret. Most law students do not get their post-graduation jobs from OCIs. This is where your extensive networking comes into play. You can use your professional experience, whether pre-law school or even during law school, to stand out from the crowd. It will likely be a little easier to network with attorneys that practice in areas of connection to your current background.

SARAH'S TIP — x

You don't have to go to a T14 law school, participate in Big Law summer associate programs, or even go through a formal application process to land a Big Law offer. It's rare, but if you have a goal of heading into Big Law, you can also get there through hard work and networking. People may tell you along the way that you don't want to do Big Law, or they may even say you won't be able to. If it's your goal, take their advice into consideration, but don't let it limit your aspirations.

12.6 Internships

Another great way to set yourself up for post-graduation success is to participate in internships. You may feel like you are at the brink and not able to add an entire internship to your plate, and we get it. But there are a variety of internships available, with some only requiring an hour per week and others that provide flexibility to do the work during semester breaks. Other internships involve much more significant time commitments. The goal is to find one that works for your life. You may simply not have the capacity to avail of an internship during law school—if that is the case, hang in there for a few more paragraphs.

You will hear it a lot, but law school teaches you the law and there are many practical skills you learn by actually practicing. Going after a variety of internships is a great way to start building a solid base of legal skills. For example, if you would like to work as in-house counsel someday, spending time working for a firm will actually help as well. Many outside counsel engage firms for specific segments of work so having firm experience in your background will be really helpful in finding outside counsel to hire and understanding their billing practices to stay in alignment with your budget.

Federal internships seem to have the most future employer appeal, so if you can secure an internship with a federal judge—do it. An appellate internship is even better, though many look for a little more experience. U.S. Supreme Court opportunities are a bit like unicorns, in that they exist and are amazing, though notoriously difficult to come by.

SARAH'S TIP — X

Career service employees should wear capes. Through a networking conversation I ended up with an opportunity to intern under a federal judge. You never know the downstream effect of a conversation, so always be professional and put your best foot forward!

Many state courts, but not all, also have internship opportunities. These are great for learning and growing. The highest court in the state will carry the most prestige, followed by appellate court, and lastly trial courts. This is not to say you should not accept a role with a trial judge if offered the opportunity; any judicial opportunity is a huge boost in your career journey for both learning and networking.

Beyond the court systems, there are also internships with firms, prosecutors, defenders, etc. The possibilities are endless. Where there is an attorney, there is a potential opportunity for an internship. Additionally, you may find an internship in an area you really enjoy even if it is not particularly designated for a law student. For example, there are many government agencies that provide internships and law students are welcome to apply as are undergraduate students. If you want to work for the federal government, or even get a boost in the private sector, understanding how government agencies work will set you apart from other candidates.

JESSICA'S STORY — x

I happened to be scrolling through social media one day and noticed a post from the National Park Service related to VSFS—Virtual Student Federal Service Internship. I checked it out, and found that there were a variety of internships including law and public policy. Looking at unusual avenues that may be tangentially related to law are always worth considering. Additionally, some of the departments may be willing to work with your interest area so that both you and their organization can get the most of the experience. For example, an EMS program may still have legal and policy issues that must be considered.

While looking for an externship and exploring firms more closely, I actually learned that some lawyers practice in fire litigation, something I had never heard of before. If you look, you may be surprised to find your other interests and passions can be successfully combined into a legal career.

If you are able to accommodate a host of internship opportunities, you will probably find internships you love, and maybe even one or two that you hate. Do not despair if you hate an internship, learn what you can from it, and when the timing is right (only you can decide that) move on. You have learned a valuable lesson in finding an area of law that is not the right fit for you. Be careful not to burn bridges on your way out, because the legal community tends to be close knit and you may cross paths again in the future. If you love an internship, congratulations! This internship is an invaluable learning experience for you and may even be a pathway to a post-graduation job offer.

SARAH'S STORY — x

I had an internship that wasn't the right fit in terms of practice area. However, through that internship I had the opportunity to help my supervising attorney prepare for oral arguments at our state supreme court. I became intimately familiar with the case and was afforded the opportunity to attend the oral arguments. This will forever be a highlight of my legal education, and it happened back in my second semester of 1L!

BETHANY'S TIP — x

These can be a lot of fun! Through connections on LinkedIn, I was able to find a role doing writing and research for an annual textbook supplement. It helped me deepen my knowledge in Tort Law, beyond what was covered in both levels in the program, and looks really good on my resume that spans both sides of my career preferences. The best part: it was fully remote and allowed me to create my own schedule.

Even if you do not participate in routine internships, many law schools offer or require externships options where students earn course credit for spending a designated number of hours under the supervision of an attorney. This is a great way to build your practical skills and earn course credit concurrently. Additionally, many law schools allow students to be paid for time spent in an externship, so it is a triple win all around.

SARAH'S TIP — x

Don't see any internship postings in your area? I was able to get an internship offer by checking out associate attorney (i.e., new grad) openings on the state bar website. I contacted a local firm that had an unfilled opening in a practice area I was interested in learning more about. An offer was extended and the rest is history . . .

If you are not sure how to get started with networking for an internship, here is a sample email for inspiration that you can modify:

> Dear [Attorney],
>
> My name is [Name], and I live here in [Locality] and am currently attending law school at [University Name] through an [ABA waiver program]. I noticed your law firm has [practice area] and I am interested in learning more about this practice area. [Insert 2 accolades about yourself.] I am wondering if your firm allows for internships or if you know of any local firms that host [spring/summer/fall] semester interns?
>
> Sincerely,
> [Name]

12.7 Clerkships

It may feel a bit premature to mention this, but clerkships are another great area to consider and are typically a post-graduation role, though some firms do hire clerks still in law school. Judicial clerkships follow the same internship advice above in terms of federal and state breakdowns and prestige. Federal clerkships are available on the OSCAR site and state clerkships are usually listed on the state's website. These are incredible roles that provide gateways to your career long term. You can expect to write bench memos and draft opinions for the judge or justice. These roles typically open to apply the year prior to graduation, so it is helpful to keep on your radar.

As a general rule of thumb, the most prestigious law firms and clerkships typically go to candidates with top academics. Also, the 1L year is typically given more weight in terms of grades than upper-level semesters. That said, if your first semester is subpar, just know there are Big Law firms and judges that take a much broader approach to hiring and have shirked elitism.

12.8 Master of Laws (LLM)

A Master of Laws degree is often referred to as an LLM. An LLM degree is an advanced law degree—think of it as an advanced concentration program that you may be adding to your JD. There are many reasons to consider an LLM, including if you are moving your practice area from overseas to the U.S., your overseas work is having increasing U.S. ties, or you want to gain more knowledge in a specific area to increase your ability to get into that practice area. If you received your legal education abroad, the LLM is a great way to position yourself to take the bar in the U.S. LLM students already licensed in the U.S. tend to pursue LLMs to enrich their knowledge base.

LLM degrees can have a large variety of concentrations, something that may have been limited in your JD program. If you suddenly learn that you want more knowledge on things like tax law, business law, international law, intellectual property law, etc. then an LLM program might be a great next step.

An LLM may be something you pursue immediately after your JD or you may wait and decide you need this additional education shortly after a major overhaul in your practice area (think a new bankruptcy or tax code that changes everything). It is never too late, and you can do it. That being said, the majority of lawyers never get a LLM since it is unnecessary in some career areas (general practice).

12.9 Legal Adjacent Fields

Legal adjacent fields were mentioned near the beginning of this chapter, but it is worth going into a little more detail about them. If you find yourself questioning why you went to law school in the first place, rest assured, this may be an area you want to explore. Most legal adjacent roles do not require bar passage; rather, they list the JD as a preference. You do not have to love trials and oral arguments to flourish in a legal adjacent role. If you ever feel like the practice of law is not a good fit, take a moment and explore these roles before making any final decisions. A JD is an extremely versatile degree that can be used for many different roles beyond the traditional practicing attorney route.

12.10 Conclusion

You may be feeling a bit overwhelmed after reading through all of that. Remember, it is only your first semester. You have plenty of time to explore, learn, and grow in a timeline that works for your life. Whether you jump into internships your first semester, your last, or do not have time during law school, you still have plenty of opportunities to prepare for your end goals.

Key Takeaways

- Take some time to explore various practice areas and practice settings.
- If you have bandwidth, jump into interning for a practical learning experience.
- Career services is a great way to get started—reach out today!

▷▷▷ 13

Fuzzies or Flames

Time for Finals

You have worked hard all semester. If you have been outlining and studying along the way, your preparation for finals will be much smoother. Rest assured, if you have procrastinated, there are still steps you can take to prepare yourself... and you may find that you never want to be in this boat again.

There are many different approaches to final exams. The first step to your preparations is to figure out what to expect by asking your professor. Here is a quick checklist of key things:

- Open book or closed book?
- How many multiple choice questions?
- How many essay questions?
- How many points are designated for each question?
- How much time is allotted? (No matter the answer, it is never enough!)
- Mid-exam break?
- Limitations: word count, character count?
- Past exams to use for practice? (Also check library website.)

13.1 Closed Book Exams

Closed book exams are the norm, and they are the perfect way to prepare for the bar. Professors tend to limit the scope of their testing to concepts taught within the course. This is great because you have all the information available to you in your textbook and lecture notes.

At a high level, multiple choice questions test on the rules whereas essays are focused on using your knowledge of the rules to analyze a fact pattern and recognize available counter points. Start by focusing on your knowledge of the rules because it is the foundational skill to prepare for both. One of the best ways to prepare for essay writing exams is by reading the explanations for multiple choice practice questions (even the ones you get right). It gets you used to seeing a fact pattern and analysis including the terms of art you will need to use in drafting your essay answer.

As a reminder, while commercial resources are great, you have to know the scope of what you are being tested on. Often supplements and sample questions include material not covered in your course. If you come across material that differs from what you remember, look it up in your outline and textbook. If it is not there, put that tidbit on the backburner for another day.

Chapter 6 covers multiple choice questions and Chapter 7 covers essay writing. If you do not feel like you have mastered those skills quite yet, circle back and walk through those chapters again.

SARAH'S TIP — x

I try to template every concept from the course I think there may be an essay for. Every single one. This helps me work through the material and identify my gaps in ways that simply practicing multiple choice questions can gloss over.

13.2 Open Book Exams

You might be thinking you hit the jackpot if you are getting an open book exam. Not to burst your bubble, but professors tend to make open book exams more difficult. They still have to curve so the difficulty is necessary to maintain the academic rigor. There is a temptation with open book exams to think that you do not need to memorize everything. Remember those essays where there is never enough time? If you spend time looking everything up, your final score will show it. Instead, you should plan to study just as much as you do for a closed book exam. Prep your materials early and use them as needed while you practice.

SARAH'S TIP

If I am prepping for an open book exam, I get all of the materials ready ahead of time. I tab my textbook and then I print my templates, print my mini-outline, and have my class notes organized by week — in that order in a binder. As I am going through practice essays and multiple choice questions, I time myself and use my resources when need be. That helps me identify areas of weakness and gets me familiar with finding things quickly in my binder or textbook.

13.3 Game Day Prep

Make a plan. Know heading into the exam how much time you want to spend on multiple choice questions and how much you want to spend on each essay. As you're making your time allocation plan, keep in mind the points for each question. Go in order and don't look back unless by some miracle you have extra time at the end and only then circle back. Even then, you may want to spend that time on refining your essay responses because essays typically have more points available than multiple choice questions.

Do not fall into the trap of thinking content tested during a midterm or previous tests will not be on the midterm. While this content may not be tested as heavily on the final, it is still important to be prepared to demonstrate your learning with just as much zeal. From our experience, concepts tested on a midterm are often also tested on the final, but from a slightly different angle. It is best to be prepared for anything!

Anxiety is real. Having 40–70% of your grade come from a single final is no small undertaking. You may find it helpful to do some meditation, exercise, or listen to your favorite playlist prior to the exam. Take a few deep breaths and get into your Zen mode.

If you are running severely behind schedule, you may want to jump into your essays if they are worth more points than individual multiple choice questions. For example, this may require you to simply click an answer on the last 3 multiple choice questions in order to start writing your essays. You likely have a 1 in 4 chance of getting the multiple choice question right simply by clicking an answer; there is no such opportunity for chance points on an essay question. If it is not written, there are no points for it. Again, only use this method if absolutely necessary and you have ended up entirely off course with your time.

If your exam is being administered through monitoring software, check to see if there is a practice test you can do ahead of the exam.

BETHANY'S TIP — x

It is possible to over-study. One semester I was "blessed" with my "favorite" type of quizzes and exams repetitively: multiple choice. It was the hardest semester to date. I started keeping track of the time I spent studying compared to what my scores were. I found that approximately 7–9 hours on a 5-point quiz gave largely better results than 10–12 hours, and slightly better results than 3–6 hours. Obviously this wasn't an official study, but it gave me good insight of approximately how much I needed to study to feel prepared, but not overwhelmed, for multiple choice based exams. Of course, this happened to be the same semester I took the MPRE, a fully multiple choice exam. Knowing how much time was needed for me to feel more confident on this style of exam helped me set a study pace throughout the semester. Good news: I passed with the ability to sit for any state.

SARAH'S STORY — x

The title for this chapter has some literal inspiration. During one of my finals, our smoke alarm went off. I never realized how many alarms we had in our house until every single one was blaring during a timed exam. Thankfully everything turned out just fine. We have a new approach: order pizza because there's no cooking allowed while I'm testing!

Key Takeaways

- The final exam is critically important because it typically constitutes the largest portion of your grade.
- Make a plan heading into the exam based upon the points available.
- Take a deep breath—you have been working hard the whole semester and you are ready for this.

▷▷▷ 14

A Note of Encouragement

If no one has told you yet, we are proud of you for taking this journey. Law school is not easy, and being online does not make it any easier. You are embarking on an experience that will be unlike any other, and many of you may never meet another lawyer who has had experience in an online program.

At some times during your experience, you may feel lost, disconnected, or even that this is not meant for you. The bottom line is if you want to be here, truly want to be part of the experience of your own accord, you can do this. You are going to be just fine.

The reality is we have all been there. Each author of this book has experienced their own rounds of feeling they were not good enough, that this semester would be their last, or that they had no true connections. In many ways, this book was a culmination to show that each of us processed and overcame challenges in a different way and we wished that we had a guide like this one that helped us recognize that what we were experiencing was normal and part of the process.

On those darkest of days, remember all of the things you have achieved. You made it into a law program in a new format that is transforming the world of and access to justice. By merely being part of the program, you are already making a difference. On the best of days, take a note (mental or physical) and keep it with you.

We hope that you will share what you have learned and how you have adapted in a modern law program by joining us on our LinkedIn pages so we can grow our community together. Please connect with us at:

Figure 14.1. Jessica's LinkedIn QR Code

Figure 14.2. Bethany's LinkedIn QR Code

Figure 14.3. Sarah's LinkedIn QR Code

Figure 14.4. Digitally Remastered's LinkedIn QR Code

Section Three

Winter Break

▷▷▷ 15

Grades and Your Self-Worth

Waiting for grades, especially after seeing some terrifying midterm grades, can be stressful. It can be hard knowing that your grade is entirely dependent on your knowledge in comparison to your classmates, which makes final grades that much harder to reconcile.

JESSICA'S TIP — x

Manage your grade expectations from the beginning. If you think you got an A, you are likely to be sorely disappointed. Look at your scores in comparison to others, be realistic, and round down.

It is often said that you are overconfident if you don't know the material, and underconfident if you know the material well. I am not suggesting that you can't be underconfident and not know the material.

Do not beat yourself up over the grades, because it does not measure self-worth. Law school grading only tests specific skills, generally your analytical and memorization skills. Successful lawyers need more than memorization. They need to be able to connect with clients, argue their client's position, and explain complex concepts in an easy to understand manner. The most eloquent speaker in class is not necessarily the best writer, and these things will not show up in an exam score.

Just because you did not get the highest score does not mean you cannot still be a great lawyer or that someone else is better than you. The tests are subjective and limited, especially for doctrinal classes. You may shine when you get to oral arguments or client counseling courses. Also, getting a low grade in a specific class does not mean that you should shy away from practicing in that area. Academic scores are an important assessment, but not dispositive of your aptitude to practice in a certain area of law.

The school may be able to give you an unofficial class ranking after your first semester. Remember that it is unofficial, and depending on the program, you may be looking at your ranking compared to students who have completed more classes and will graduate before you. A more accurate ranking may take longer than a traditional program, where 1L is completed in two semesters, if your program extends 1L beyond two semesters. Many law schools will rank you against the residential students graduating at the same time as you.

Once grades come out, there will inevitably be discussions about how you did, and even people you do not regularly talk to will ask. Only share what you are comfortable with, and if you do share, set expectations regarding confidentiality. People will ask because they want to know how people rank, to find other people who are having the same issues and experiences they are having, or (for the competitive ones) to determine who the competition is with regards to grades.

JESSICA'S TIP — x

If you feel pressured to discuss grades, you can be vague. It also keeps you from unnecessarily rubbing it in if you find the exams easy and are getting top marks. Remember, even if you are getting the top grades, your work was not perfect and there is still room for improvement. Some possible responses: "I did better than I expected, but not perfect." "There is room for improvement." "I was hoping to do better." "It was harder than I expected."

If your grades are lower than you expected, you may want to consider your exam performance and the possibility that you need an accommodation. Although you may have never needed one before, law school produces a lot of anxiety, and can cause issues that you have always worked around to become insurmountable. The tightly timed exams can mean that a slower reading time caused by undiagnosed dyslexia is now an issue when it never caused an issue in undergrad. If you think an accommodation might be needed, you will want to start this process early, and your free time during break may be the perfect time to try to schedule those appointments. We covered this in detail back in Chapter 5 and would encourage you to circle back and refresh on the content if you think you may need an accommodation.

If you excelled your first semester and ended up with top scores, congratulations, we are so proud of you! Even if you scored well and are happy with your grades, you may still need to make adjustments for the next semester because your peers are going to continue to push themselves and grow in their skills. Do not fall into the trap of complacency and get left in the dust. Also, if you are a lucky duck doing well, consider if you have bandwidth to help a peer or two that are struggling. If you can explain it to others, it is a great way to make sure you understand it yourself, so it is a two-for-one deal—you get to be a nice human and maintain your performance.

BETHANY'S STORY — x

Some of the best advice I've received since starting law school is that it's OK to take a different path. There is this societal pressure in law school that your goal should be top of the class, be invited to law review, and spend every non-classroom minute studying ... Surprise! That literally cannot be everyone's end result. And it might be your goal to start, but you could change it along the way. I wanted to be successfully and gainfully employed full-time, maintain a healthy marriage, and hold internships in areas I was interested in. Balancing that with being top of the class didn't happen. It's a give and take, so don't underestimate how much time relationships or other involvement is going to take. Law school, even part-time, is like another full-time job.

I have had some of the best experiences with internships that allow me to work directly within my passion for the ADA and writing for textbooks. I have been able to participate in committee work at my place of employment that directly ties into my passion for higher education policy. There are ways to still shine on your resume when you're not top of the class. And these are things that stand out because I had to go out of my way to find and create these opportunities.

At first, I felt like I was doing something wrong. If I didn't get straight A's, I wasn't meant to be a lawyer. If I don't get invited to law review, I'll never have published work in the field. I've said this before and will say it again: if you want to be there, you are meant to be there. Grades do not determine your career. (They might influence it, but they do not determine it!) Maybe the top percentage of the class don't feel this way—but I have a hunch that most of the rest of the class does. Find your path to success, whatever it may be, and continue confidently on that path.

15.1 Imposter Syndrome

Even decent grades may result in imposter syndrome, because you may ask yourself why your classmate who works twice as hard as you is struggling when you are not. This will lead you to doubt your achievements and wonder if you are just getting good grades by luck, especially if you do not always feel confident with your knowledge of the material.

Imposter syndrome, regardless of grades, can be a very real concern for students. Imposter syndrome is when you doubt your abilities and accomplishments and fear that people will find out you are a fraud. Despite the fact that most law schools inevitably drop students if their GPAs are too low, law schools do not accept students if they do not think there is a possibility that the student will be able to succeed in the program. If your grades are lower than you expected, you may be more inclined to feel like you do not belong in law school, but we promise you do. Something in your background demonstrated to the school that you have the potential to be a great lawyer.

What is not healthy is name-calling, creating false rumors behind people's backs, and making insinuations when you have no evidence. Eventually classmates will see through it, and it will affect how you are perceived. Since law school is the start of your professional identity, you do not want these behaviors to give you an early perception as a possibly unscrupulous lawyer.

Law school is filled with high achievers, and we get it, you want to do well. Some of you may have even chosen law school because you like to compete and win, but are not cut out for professional sports. Tone it down with your classmates. We guarantee no one came into the program wanting to fail, so do not add extra pressure. Sometimes a little healthy competition is good, but you can focus that energy on improving your grades and excelling in ABA competitions or moot court.

JESSICA'S TIP — x

I spend a lot of my time doubting my abilities, especially when I struggle with networking (a known weakness of mine). It can be a very personal struggle with no real cause beyond fear.

SARAH'S TIP — x

I had imposter syndrome hard during an internship with Ivy League peers. It was intimidating, but I realized that I had the skills to keep up. We're all learning the same principles and will take the same bar exam, so don't let labels or pompous attitudes dim your sparkle.

BETHANY'S TIP — x

It is easy to slip into the cycle of self-doubt when you're only seeing your scores without context or peers are posting their law-related successes on social media. Remember that a raw score only tells half the story without the curve, and social media posts never seem to focus on the negative. It is extremely beneficial when professors post ranges/curves early on so you have an objective starting point when assessing your progress.

15.2 Scheduling

Winter break is a great time to reflect on what worked well for you in the first semester and what, if anything, needs to change moving forward. Take a little time to think about your first semester of law school. It might have been a dumpster fire, it may have been like floating on a cloud (in which case, you are a unicorn and we are jealous), or it may have been something in between.

If your grades are not quite what you were hoping for, semester break is the perfect time to recalibrate. For example, you may find that you spent too much of your available time case briefing and that you need to dedicate more time to rules memorization. You may find scheduling additional time with professors to review your questions actually makes your study time more productive.

If you had stellar performance and are happy with your grades, you may still need to revisit your schedule for spring. Different courses require different levels of attention. You may encounter a subject that does not come as naturally to you and need to dedicate more time to mastering the material. Law school semesters do not tend to be "one size fits all" so it is important to adjust your approach along the way to maintain top performance.

You may need to use a formal to-do list or change up the mix to implement a more effective to-do list method. Time blocking out your schedule and maintaining dedicated segments of time to focus on law school can also greatly aid in your efforts for the next semester. There are many great gems in Chapter 5 as well, so circle back for a deeper dive if needed.

A key note to remember is that law schools often allow students to take a lighter course load after they have completed 1L. If your scheduling is not working out, you may need to reach out to the administration. Before making any final decisions, spend time reviewing all of the solutions available to you.

15.3 Personal Life & Career

Perhaps you have identified that you need to have better balance with your personal life or you would like to add an internship into the mix. It may be as simple as dedicating an hour or two each week for "me time," date night, or dedicated time with the kiddos. Everyone's life is different, so the focus is finding what works for you as an individual.

You may find vacationing during the semester works better for you because you need to use your semester breaks as downtime. Pro tip: If you find that you are a semester vacationer try to avoid midterms and finals at all costs. The start of the semester or just after midterms is usually the best time to jet out of town. Conversely, you may find that you need to schedule vacations during semester breaks. Having a vacation planned can be a great carrot to help drive motivation to finish the semester strong.

You may also find that continuing in your current career does not work well with the needs of your educational journey and personal life. It may work for you to adjust to part-time or step into a different role with more flexibility. Internships are a great way to start building on your practical skills and generally have flexibility for law students around midterms and finals. Your life needs may not support a career change during law school. For example, it may be cost prohibitive to make an adjustment at this point in time. You might also find it helpful to revisit Chapter 12.

After you have reflected upon the changes you need to make for the next semester, take a moment and write down your changes and associated goals. Congratulations, you have made your first big step towards academic success next semester.

SARAH'S TIP — x

As a mom, I am juggling a lot during the semester. I always try to schedule dentist appointments, doctor appointments, veterinary appointments, car oil changes, etc. during my breaks. During semester breaks, I repurpose my study blocks for these appointments to make sure I am heading into the next semester with as few distractions as possible.

Key Takeaways

- Grades do not measure your self-worth.
- Regardless of GPA, you are getting the same degree as your peers.
- If you are unhappy with your grade, reflect on what is and is not working and make the necessary changes. Evaluate if you would benefit from an accommodation.
- If you are happy with your grades, do not become complacent. Keep pushing and reflect on whether you have bandwidth to help other students that are struggling.

▷▷▷ 16

Preface to Professionality

Professionalism is an ever-changing idea in society. There is no doubt that there are still negative historical ties to how this shows up in the legal field. We have intentionally left some more well-known areas of professionalism out due to their ties to identity, especially areas where only you can make the best decision (i.e., professional dress on video conferences). However, we have done our best to identify the most important elements in this area that are relevant to your online experience and encourage you to adopt them in ways that personally empower you.

16.1 Finding a Mentor & Networking

Take a moment to reflect on the following scenario:

You had a difficult day. There was something going on at work and your colleague made a decision that does not make sense. You also got news that your favorite aunt is in the hospital, the same hospital that called you today about those results you have been dreading about your recent blood work. Do not forget, you still have some reading to finish up before class tonight because you are likely on call, and you still have to figure out how to fit in an internship at some point this semester.

Are you stressed yet? We are.

Who would you go to after a day like this one? Likely, you would have a few folks up your sleeve, and not one singular person for all of these. For some of these things, you probably have a friend you can go to to rant or gossip about how that work decision really just caused even more work for you. However, is that the same person you would go to to make a plan to change jobs due to that decision? What about getting advice on how to balance giving homecare to your hospitalized aunt while going to school and finding an internship within your new-found passion of disability law?

Even if you have never explicitly called someone a mentor previously, you have probably had experience with mentorship before. Who have you sought out to ask questions about how they have managed situations previously? Mentors are the folks in your life who can share their experiences and the wisdom learned on the path they have taken. It does not have to be an identical path to yours, but similar enough that you can gain some insight from their experiences. Having a strong network of mentors is essential to being successful in an online law program.

But how can you have mentors in a program modality that is so new? Glad you asked. To address the online portion, there are folks who have already graduated, or are closer to graduating, from an online program; connect with them. Perhaps you are in a newer program and are part of the first cohort of students; in that case, connect with another online program. Luckily, your online program is not just about online law school. Find those mentors who share(d) other stressors with you and connect, even if they were not in an online program. Many lawyers, due to COVID, have had at least some experience in an online space and can still provide great mentorship for what you are experiencing.

Also note: A mentor and a boss are similar to a rectangle and a square. They can be the same person, but likely are not. A mentor is someone who gives advice and does not necessarily have any stake in your success—other than a good mentorship relationship. A boss, however, has a direct power-based relationship over you and does have a stake in your success. A mentor can help you develop your professional identity holistically, whereas a boss may be more focused on your development within your particular role. This line can be a gray one, but we highly suggest having at least one mentor who is not also a boss.

16.2 Securing a Mentor

One of the quickest ways to secure a mentor is through the wide net approach. Put a status on social media with what you are looking for in a mentor, including what background you would prefer they share, and see who bites. Stranger things have happened, and there are a lot of great folks who are looking to mentor.

However, you might be looking for a very specific mentorship area, or maybe your social media is not up to snuff and you just are not connected to the right folks. This is when networking comes in. If you have not yet created a LinkedIn, this is your subliminal messaging. Put this book down and do it, right now. While you are at it, be sure to connect with the three authors of this book to build your network! To do a targeted approach, you are going to need to be OK with "no." Say it to yourself in a mirror, practice asking friends outrageous things they will definitely disagree with, read a self-help book, whatever it takes. A "no" is not the end of the world, merely a diversion to take a different path.

Another approach is one that is a bit more targeted. Start reaching out to folks who share similar interests as you that you are connected with already. Ask them questions about their journey, and always ask them who they think you should speak with next. This may take a few rounds to get to a person who specifically focuses on what you are looking for, but it is said we are only six degrees away from being connected to anyone. Chances are, within six meetings, you have probably found someone who would be a great fit.

But how do you make it official? Honestly, it is up to the two of you whether being official is something you need. Some mentor/mentee relationships are never official and have an unstated understanding of the roles. However, most successful partnerships are founded on a more official ask and an understanding of what the partners need from one another. After all, if the mentee is expecting to meet every week but the mentor only has enough time to send an email every third month, this might not be the best match. We suggest asking the person directly once you establish there is a good fit and then establishing joint expectations.

JESSICA'S TIP — x

I have been told how many lawyers want to work with you and help you. Despite this, be prepared for no response or a no when you reach out. I have stopped in to set up a short lunch with multiple firms where I either knew the partners or had heard very positive things about the lawyers and never heard anything back from them.

BETHANY'S TIP — x

If you're looking for a good book on getting over rejection, I would strongly encourage Jia Jang's *Rejection Proof: How I Beat Fear and Became Invincible, One Rejection At a Time.* It's a quick and funny read, and truly gets to the heart of why we're so afraid of "no."

16.3 I Have a Mentor, What Next?

Set those expectations and meet your end of the bargain, too. Establish what you need out of the relationship. Are you wanting them to give you reading suggestions, tell about their personal experience, or connect you with their peers? Do you want to meet monthly over coffee or each semester at a local conference? There is no one-size-fits-all in this category, and your wants and needs will probably change as you change mentors.

Be prepared. Come prepared to your meeting with your mentors with questions. There is nothing more embarrassing than arriving at a meeting and sitting in silence because you expect them to just pour knowledge into your brain, especially on Zoom. What are you wanting to learn about their experience? What did you notice about their resume on LinkedIn that sparked your interest? What is something you are struggling with that you think they might be able to offer feedback on? And if they asked you to come prepared with a reading to discuss or thoughts on a recent occurrence, please do not wait until five minutes prior to start it. Your mentor's time is valuable; they are not there to help you formulate your decision, but to think about your decisions critically.

Take their advice and chew on it later. What does that mean? It means during your time together, soak in everything they are sharing. Even if you do not agree with it on face value. Then, after the meeting, spend time to reflect on what has been shared and toss the stuff you do not need. There will be times in a moment of advice that we are emotional, but when we are in a critical thinking mode it seems to make more sense or be perceived differently. Make time to reflect in a calm state. You will probably even end up with conflicting advice at some point. It is not your job to change their mind; you are there to learn from others so you can further develop your own definitions and journeys.

Keep looking. You should have more than one mentor. A singular person cannot possibly be an expert in all things law or human. Continue to connect with folks. It is OK to have more than one person to go to when you have a question. After all, those scientists seem to have a pretty great method for getting accurate results ... Just do not spread yourself so thin that you are unable to uphold your role as a mentee. And, if you find it is not a good fit, it is also OK to excuse yourself from the relationship. It is a good thing to outgrow a mentor, because it shows you have grown—hopefully with their guidance. And if not, at least you have learned how not to be a mentor to your future mentees.

SARAH'S TIP — x

I have been really fortunate to connect with numerous mentors and value each one. Some state bars have formal mentoring programs, but I have preferred a more fluid approach without the constraint of formality. The key is finding a dynamic that works for both parties.

16.4 Networking in the Online World

Networking does not just have to be for mentorship, and it can be a bit different when you are in an online program. Your career services office is not down the physical hallway from you, and you are not passing the job fairs on your way to class. However, there are still resources to help you succeed in this avenue.

Utilize career services. You might not be able to be there in person, but we have yet to meet an office that refuses to meet online. Many universities also offer online job boards. Practice online interviews and participate in resume review sessions whenever they are offered by your school.

Additionally, your professors are a great resource. If they mention having a background in an area of law you are interested in, ask for them to connect you with someone from their past. Even if they do not have experience in a specific area, they can help connect you with local bars and conferences that could be that perfect connector.

Lastly, use the physical network that is near you. Even if you live hundreds or thousands of miles away from your law school, you probably have some kind of bar or firm that is local to you. Make a phone call, send an email, or stop by in person to make a connection. You might find yourself not only a mentor, but an internship or job offer along the way.

BETHANY'S STORY — x

Honestly, if it weren't for networking, who knows if this book would be in existence! This idea of a book had been floating in our minds for a semester or so, but we had no background in publishing. I am a member of many Facebook groups geared toward law school, and I noticed someone posting about their book. I reached out on a whim to see if they would speak to our team about the publishing process as fellow female lawyers-to-be, and boom! Here we are. We still keep in contact, and I am so thankful to have them in my network.

JESSICA'S STORY — x

This person isn't necessarily a mentor, but a lawyer I have always respected in my area. A semester and a half into law school, I reached out to his office to see if he would meet with me and talk to me about the legal profession. He let me pick his brain for over an hour about the legal field, especially in our state. Be prepared to have your brain picked too! He was just as interested in my experience with online legal education as I was in finding out more about the legal field.

BETHANY'S TIP — x

I started by navigating to my local bar's LinkedIn page and started connecting with all of the lawyers who were listed. This took me days, but it filled my feed with so many different opportunities and potential employers. Since doing this, I have had more connection calls and emails than I can count, and they have led to more internships and additional connections directly in the field of law I hope to focus in.

16.5 Professional Responsibility

A very important area within the legal profession is professional responsibility. Mentors are uniquely positioned to help you grow in your professional identity, including your approach to practicing ethically. As you are meeting with your mentor, consider asking them about their approach to professional responsibility through practicing ethically.

Each state enacts their own ethics rules, which is a pretty common theme amongst the states that you will encounter throughout law school. Although states tend to base their code of conduct on the ABA's Model Rules of Professional Conduct, the state's rules may align with an earlier version of the ABA's Model Rules or have been adopted with variations from the ABA's Model Rules.[1] Even as a law student, you will want to familiarize yourself with your jurisdiction's rules before you start an internship, work for a firm, or even talk to family and friends about different areas of law.

Within an internship setting, your supervising attorney will be able to help guide your development of ethical standards. Many of the model rules discuss conflicts of interest. The comment for ABA Model Rule 1.10 mentions that work done as a law student can create conflicts that could require you to be screened.[2] You should talk to your supervising attorney about whether or not you need to keep a list of clients you've worked on during your internship for future conflicts checks.

ABA Model Rule 5.5 covers the unauthorized practice of law. Only licensed attorneys are permitted to practice law.[3] As you begin to develop your legal knowledge throughout law school, it can be tempting to weigh in on things and help your friends and family. Moreover, you may have people coming out of the woodworks to ask you questions. Until you firmly understand the unauthorized practice of law in your jurisdiction, it is best to hold off from providing any legal input. You probably do not have sanctions on your bucket list.

Knowing and practicing under the guidance of these model rules is essential to preventing a malpractice claim. A malpractice claim can harm your reputation as a lawyer and prevent a future career in law. A claim of

1. *See* Model Rules of Pro. Conduct (Am. Bar Ass'n 2021).
2. Model Rules of Pro. Conduct r. 1.10 (Am. Bar Ass'n 2021).
3. Model Rules of Pro. Conduct r. 5.5 (Am. Bar Ass'n 2021).

"not knowing" what you were doing was wrong will not save you from a malpractice claim, so be sure to review these rules early on in your legal journey.

16.6 MPRE

The MPRE is an important step towards becoming a licensed attorney. MPRE stands for Multistate Professional Responsibility Examination.[4] Many law students take the MPRE prior to graduating law school, but some choose to wait to take the MPRE until after taking the bar exam.

The MPRE is based upon the ABA's Model Rules of Professional Responsibility and is purely a multiple choice exam.[5] The MPRE is designed to make sure you have a baseline of required ethics.[6] Notably, the exam is not about finding the most ethical answer, it is about demonstrating that you know the minimum required ethics in any given situation.

Many vendors offer a free MPRE prep course. You could sign up for several MPRE prep courses from various vendors and use it as an opportunity to decide which vendor's program approach you like the most and use that vendor for your bar prep course.

JESSICA'S TIP — x

The MPRE tends to heavily test based upon the comments. It's not enough to read the rules; the comments to each rule are just as important.

The great news is that the ABA Model Rules and associated comments are fully available online. You can order a book if that is more your speed, or you can access the rules for free on the ABA's website.

Many states have adopted verbiage from the ABA's Model Rules of Professional Responsibility; however, there may be some nuanced differences in your state. It is not unheard of for a state's model rules to be based on an earlier version of the ABA's Model Rules. The MPRE is based upon the ABA's

4. National Conference of Bar Examiners, *Multistate Professional Responsibility Examination*, https://www.ncbex.org/exams/mpre/ (last visited Oct. 30, 2014).

5. *Id.*

6. *Id.*

model rules, so it is important to spend a little time getting familiar with the requirements of your jurisdiction. You will need to check with your state bar association to make sure you are following the correct rules for your jurisdiction.

Key Takeaways

- Having a mentor is great for becoming well-rounded and learning about practice areas of interest.
- Developing your professional identity includes developing your ethical standards.
- The MPRE tests your knowledge of ethics with respect to the practice of law and is usually taken by law students prior to graduation.

Appendices

▷▷▷ APPENDIX A

When You Come to Campus

Some of your programs may require you to physically visit campus. Not being in a traditional residential program can mean a steep learning curve initially. We are providing the following tips to help lessen the stress of this change in space and schedule.

For the Classroom

The primary reason for a trip to campus is for the class time. Make sure that you receive a schedule with ample time prior to your trip. You need to know which classes you will be attending while on campus and what is required for those classes.

For each class, check the requirements for:

(1) Outfits: Is it casual, or courtroom attire?
(2) Books: Do you need all the textbooks, or can you limit it to select chapters or books (when you have multiple)?
(3) Any special presentation materials?

Also, even if you are an entirely digital person and do all your notes on a laptop or tablet, bring a pen. A professor will undoubtedly give you a paper handout or you will need to fill out some type of form for the school.

SARAH'S TIP — x

If you're flying, never check your bag. Law school textbooks are expensive and you don't want to lose them in a lost luggage situation!

JESSICA'S TIP

If you are traveling to school, make sure you have already downloaded apps and set up any accounts you may need on your phone. If you live in a remote area that does not have or use services like Lyft, Uber, and Venmo, you might need to set accounts up for your time on campus.

BETHANY'S TIP

Do not be afraid to reach out to the professors ahead of time and ask not only what materials are needed for the entire trip, but also for each day. You might only need a single copy of three cases rather than all three textbooks, depending on the schedule. That can make a huge difference in the weight you're physically carrying on your shoulders! And don't forget a backpack or other bag to tote the materials between classes.

Housing, Travel & Amenities

How are you getting to campus? If you live within a few hours of campus, it's likely a no-brainer: you are driving and possibly even commuting home every night. If you are further away you need to weigh options between driving, flying, or other methods like a train or bus. There is a certain level of ease and convenience to having your own car, and maybe you can pick up a nearby friend along the way to split gas expenses and drive time. On the other hand, by flying you can actually devote your travel time to studying and preparing schoolwork on the way to campus. This is particularly helpful if you get a last-minute 100+ page reading assignment for class.

If you fly, how will you get around town during your time on campus? A rental car is nice and several of you can pool together during your travels, but depending on the cost, using a rideshare app or public transportation may make more sense. If your campus has a room block at a particular hotel, there may even be a shuttle between the airport and hotel, and, at least during your campus visit, between the hotel and campus. The negative of relying on public transportation and shuttles is that you are confined to their schedules and cannot easily make your own plans and go where you want.

JESSICA'S TIP — x

When flying, make sure you pack any schoolwork that you can do under the seat in front of you to make the most of your time.

The university may have partnerships in place with local hotels that provide a discount on the room rates. Usually there is a block of rooms and these must be reserved within a certain window of time to take advantage of the discount. Many law students tap into these discount rooms so you get to see all your besties at breakfast and around the lobby.

You might also enjoy renting a house for you and several friends to stay in. It is a great way to make closer connections and have access to a kitchen for some healthy meals. Bonus points if you can find one within walking distance to campus.

Alternatively, if you are more introverted and need time to recharge after a full day of class with your peers, you may want to avoid the group house and main hotels. You can opt for a solo rental situation or even stay at a hotel a little further from campus to avoid the crowds. Campus visits tend to be dense periods of learning and it is OK to take a step back if you need to.

If you will have a car or other vehicle on campus, be sure to plan ahead. Take note of where the closest parking is to your classes, and whether there are any parking fees. If you are hoping to maximize your budget, you can also try to locate nearby street parking without meters. Additionally, your program may offer free or low-cost, short-term parking passes. Be sure to plan ahead if you are driving from off-campus so you can add in travel time from your vehicle to the building and your classes. Some parking lots are fifteen minutes or more away from the campus buildings. If this is a difficulty for you, communicate early with your program to request accommodations for closer parking or other arrangements for transportation to and from your parking location.

JESSICA'S TIP — x

If you are staying with a classmate, especially one you haven't stayed with before, discuss and manage expectations. Be clear if you have set sleeping/study times, want to have other classmates over to chat, or any special health/dietary restrictions.

BETHANY'S TIP — x

If you are local, there can be benefits to staying on or near campus, as well as staying at home. Personally, I prefer to save money and commute the same distance I would for my typical drive to work. This does limit the ability to attend late-evening gatherings, but we're usually pretty tired after the final class anyway. The drives can be great for audiobook review of your cases and materials.

Accommodations

Although we took a deeper dive into accommodations in Chapter 5, it is worth noting that your needed accommodations may change for an in-person experience compared to your traditional online experience. Take time to review your in-person schedule thoroughly and make note of anything that may cause a difficulty for you. Whether it is a physical limitation for parking as mentioned above, a dietary restriction if you are required to eat on campus, or even just being in person in general, accommodations are still available to you. Again, communicate early and often to ensure your needs are met.

Resources

Many universities offer resources to students within the community. It would be helpful to know of these resources prior to visiting the campus. For example, there may be a way to get reduced fares on ride shares, discounts bicycle rentals, etc. Also, many local restaurants around college campuses give student discounts. Grab your student I.D. and hit the town! This is a great list to have handy as you are planning your trip.

Relationships & Bonding

If you have orientation and a few weeks of classes online prior to meeting your classmates in person for the first time, you already have a feel for who you are close with. Do not let this limit you! If the school has organized group events, even if it is just breakfast or dinner, go to them. Sit with one person you are comfortable with or already know, but also several people you do not know well, in order to facilitate getting to know more of your peers.

Find out other people's schedules to see if anyone is on the same flight, or is arriving early or staying later. This gives you an opportunity to meet, socialize, and learn about each other. Maybe the group will plan a trip to dinner or a bar together after class one night. You can learn a lot about a person outside of a classroom setting.

JESSICA'S STORY — x

My first on-campus experience I stayed with two classmates I had never met before. I arrived at our Airbnb first and waited for them to arrive. We stayed up until well past three in the morning, much later than any of us had planned, just getting to know each other. On a side note, you will have at least one classmate who will surprise you. Despite having no justification for guessing people's height online, you will assume someone tall is short or vice versa and be shocked when you actually meet them.

BETHANY'S TIP — x

Go to the impromptu happenings. You will learn more about your colleagues in those times than all of your class time together.

And I echo Jessica's advice. Everyone always seems taller in real life. Or maybe we're just shorter!

▷▷▷ APPENDIX B

Sample Student Outlines and Templates

There are many ways to outline and prepare a template for a course. Find what works for you and make adjustments as needed. Please see below for a comparison of different versions of templates and outlines for the same classes. You will notice that these were taken from our notes exactly, so we have purposely left in spelling errors, shorthand references, and vague descriptors. Please note that these may not line up exactly with the needs of your classes. Be sure to prepare your own notes and reference the specific cases mentioned by your professors.

Torts: Sample A: Attack/Condensed Outline Format

I. Personal Torts NOTE: Transferred intent possible between battery, assault, false imprisonment, trespass to land, and trespass to chattel

   A. Battery

   B. Assault

   C. False Imprisonment

   - Defense: Shopkeeper's Privilege—*exclusive to False Imprisonment*

   D. Intentional Infliction of Emotional Distress (IIED)

II. Personal Tort Defenses

   A. Self Defense—Non Lethal Force (affirmative defense) No retreat needed

B. Self Defense—Lethal Force (affirmative defense)

C. Defense of Others (affirmative defense)

D. Consent

- Actual: Implicit or Explicit; does not need to be communicated
- Apparent
  - Not liable if:
    - A reasonable person would believe party consented
    - Custom of community are considered
- Lack of Consent (P must prove)
- Effective: Consent was to a particular conduct or substantially same
- Implied by Law: Situation implies contact is consented to

E. Informed Consent (medical specific)

- Elements:
  - Physician failed to inform adequately of material risk, and alternatives before consent
  - Patient would not consent if risks were known
  - The unknown risk occurred, and there was injury caused by the treatment
- Material risk can be determined with the standards:
  - Reasonable patient
  - Local community custom of doctors
  - Actual patient
- Defenses of Informed Consent:
  - The patient knew the risk
  - Full disclosure was detrimental to the patient's best interests
  - It was an emergency which required prompt treatment and the patient was not in a condition to decide

F. Consent Invalidated by Fraud

G. Consent Invalidated by Duress: Constraint of another's will; Spectrum:

- Physical Harm (to self or family): consent is invalidated
- Economic (i.e. job): may be invalidated in some cases
- Relationship: Consent typically still valid

H. Consent Invalidated by Lack of Capacity/Incapacitation

- Examples: Age (under 18), Severe intellectual disability, Extreme intoxication

I. Defense of land or chattel "Property" (affirmative defense)

J. Legal Authority

K. In loco parentis: acting in place of a parent (ex: teacher, full-time caregiver, not babysitter)

III. Property Torts

A. Trespass To Land

B. Trespass to Chattel (Personal Property)

- Elements
- Liability if (factor, only need one)

C. Conversion (owner's rights interfered w/ enough require pymt of full value)

IV. Property Tort Defenses

A. Private Necessity (affirmative defense)

- Liability: still exists for damage.

B. Public Necessity (affirmative defense)

- No Liability for necessary dmg; no unnecessary dmg

C. Intrusion of Land & Chattel

D. Recovery of Chattel

E. Legal Authority (same as in II.J.)

NEGLIGENCE

The Two Questions of Negligence:

1. Was the defendant negligent? (A + B)
2. Is the defendant's negligence actionable? (C + D + E)

ABC'S OF NEGLIGENCE

A. Defendant **owed a duty of care to plaintiff**

a. Duty is to act reasonably so as not to cause harm to others.

b. Standards of Conduct for Children

c. **Five characteristics of the reasonable man**

- Uses caution such a man of ordinary prudence would observe
- Cannot use substandard skill or knowledge as an excuse
- Responsible for specialized skills or knowledge possessed.
- May act differently in emergency situations (may include lesser standard of care)
- Follows customary practices but sometimes may be reasonable not to do so.

B. Defendant **breached the duty owed to plaintiff**

a. Learned Hand Test B=PxL

b. Negligence Per Se—from a statute

c. Res Ipsa Loquitur (if you do not know who actually caused harm) treated as: Matter of Law, Presumption, Inference

C. Plaintiff was **harmed**

D. Defendants breach was the **actual/factual cause of the plaintiff's harm** (But-For Test)

a. Types of Actual Causation: Joint and several liability, Concerted action, Alternative liability, & Res Ipsa Loquitur

E. Defendant's breach was the **proximate / legal cause of plaintiff's harm.**

a. Foreseeable harm

b. Rescue Doctrine

c. Superseding and intervening cause

d. Thin Skull Rule—Reasonably foreseeable that someone could be a child or older person

Limited Duty

- No duty to rescue if didn't create risk
- If you create the danger, you have the duty to protect/minimize harm
- Categorical exception to no duty: Doctor/Patient; Parent/Child, etc

- Affirmative Duty—start/say will, must complete
  - The person is imperiled and helpless/unable to protect self duty to exercise reasonable care while they are in your charge
  - Must use reasonable care
- Emotional Distress
  - Impact Zone
  - Zone of Danger
  - Bystander Rule
  - Special Relationship: Corpse, Genetic Material, Doctor/patient
- Contract
  - Exculpatory
  - Contract of Adhesion

Affirmative Defenses

1. Contributory
   a. Last Clear Chance Doctrine
2. Comparative
   a. Pure
   b. Modified
   c. Slight-Gross
   d. Barker Doctrine—illegal/criminal activity precludes liability
3. Assumption of Risk
   a. Primary Implied
   b. Express
      i. Adhesion Contract: Unconscionable—Take advantage of unequal power
      ii. Exculpatory Contract
         1. Can waive negligent but not reckless behavior
         2. Reckless is intentionally acting with disregard to safety
   c. Secondary
4. Avoidable Consequences

a. Duty to mitigate dmg: go to therapy, don't refuse treatment, must act reasonably

Landowners

1. Types
    a. Categories
        i. Trespasser
        ii. Licensee
        iii. Invitee
    b. Courts look at as a single type, dichotomy, or trichotomy
    c. Attractive Nuisance
    d. Duty to Children Trespassers
2. Firefighter Rule/First Responder/Emergency Responder Rule
3. Recreational Use
4. Outside the Premises
5. Lessors/Landlord
6. Securing against Crime

Torts: Sample B: Full-Length Torts Outline

INTENTIONAL TORTS

- Civil, citizen/corporate where someone was wronged
- Seeking damages in remedy
  - Compensation
  - Injunction: prohibit happening in the future
- single/dual intent

Intent

- Intent can be found even if:
  - negligent/reckless (Garratt v Dailey)
  - Unintended victim (Braska v Scherzer) (Talmage v Smith)
  - Is a child (Bailey v C.S.)
  - Done in good faith (Ranson v Kitner)
  - Is mentally disabled (Polmatier v Russ)
  - During horseplay (Kelley v County of Monmouth)
- But NOT if:
  - For medical examinations (Walters v Sortano)
  - Substantially certain to happen at "sometime" (has to be specific to person AND action

Battery

1. in/direct contact to P was made
   a. Plate P was holding counts
2. D made the contact
3. Contact was harmful or offensive
   b. Harmful: bodily physical harm
   c. Offensive:
      i. Offends a reasonable sense of personal dignity
      ii. Offender knows it will be highly offensive to a highly sensitive person
      iii. Generalized paranoia does not meet standard of reasonable
4. D intended action

a. Even if child (see intent above)

Medical Battery (malpractice)

1. With information, would have declined consent, AND
2. Treatment caused injury

Doctors are sued instead of hospitals (independent contractors), unless:

- *Respondeat superior, or*
- *When doing research*

Reasonable Dr v. Reasonable Patient: not all courts agree on which standard

Respondeat Superior (Business held responsible for employee's actions)

- Authorized the action or manner of the action [or]
- Agent was unfit and recklessly employed [or]
- Managerial role acting in scope of employment [or]
    - Performing work assigned
    - Course of conduct subject a control
    - Within "scope of employment" (job description)
- Employer or manager approved the act

Assault

1. P anticipates IMMINENT contact
    a. Subjective standard UNLESS based solely on actor's words (then objective standard)
    b. Does not override legal def of offensive contact
    c. Definition: occur without significant delay, not next week or "some time", think immediate
2. harmful/offensive
    a. Harmful: physical injury
    b. Offensive: offensive to the common person OR intentionally offensive to someone sensitive about a topic
3. Caused by D
    a. This is the actually person who made it happen

4. D intended contact or apprehension of
    a. See intent above

False Imprisonment

1. P is confined
    a. Physical barriers, physical force or threat of, duress, assertion of legal authority, threatens to harm Ps family or retain Ps property, P would face significant burden if left
2. P is aware/harmed
    a. Cannot be sleeping or turned the other other unaware
3. Caused by D
    a. See cause above
4. D intended
    a. See intent above

Shopkeeper's Privilege

- Reasonable belief person has stolen or attempted to
    - doesn't matter if actually did
- Detained for reasonable time
    - 10–15 minutes was deemed reasonable
- Detained in reasonable manner
    - Things to think about: do they feel as though they cannot get out of room? Locked door? Handcuffed? etc

Intentional Infliction of Emotional Distress (IIED)

1. P suffered emotional distress
    a. Typically associated with physical signs of anxiety and stress such as vomitting
2. P's emotional distress was severe
    a. Standard of no reasonable person could be expected to endure it or can no longer function
    b. Does not include depression, nervousness, vulnerability to emotional distress
3. D's extreme AND outrageous conduct caused

a. Does not include: insults, indignities, threats, annoyances, abusive language, menacing fashion of action
b. Does include causing a person to lose job for 2 years

4. D intended to cause
   a. Only intentional tort that includes reckless disregard as option for intent
   b. Even if transferred intent

Trespass to Land

1. D enters land
   a. Can be self, an object, another person, or even remains beyond consented time, or leaves something behind
2. P possessed the land
   a. Doesn't have to own! (i.e. renting)
3. D intends to enter the land
   a. Doesn't need to intend to harm it, or intend to enter x's land—just intend to enter the land in general
4. D lacked consent/privilege
   a. apparent / inferred

Trespass to Chattel

1. D dispossesses/uses/intermeddles with chattel
   a. Chattel: anything that is not real property (think not real estate)
   b. Trees/shrubs/etc: change from real property to chattel once they are cut etc
2. Chattel is possessed by P
   a. Again, ownership does not necessarily matter
3. D intends to dispossess/use/intermeddle with the chattel
   a. See intent portion above
4. D lacked consent/privilege
   a. apparent/ inferred

*D pays only the value of harm

Conversion

1. D exercises dominion/control
   a. Degree of interference matters from trespass to chattel compared to conversion
      i. extent/duration of control: how long did they have it
      ii. Intent to assert a right: see intent above
      iii. Good faith: even if didnt mean to do harm
      iv. extent/duration of resulting interference: outcomes
      v. Harm done to chattel: change of character or lost etc
      vi. Inconvenience and expense: harm to owner instead of chattel
2. P possessed the chattel
   a. Ownership doesn't necessarily matter
3. D intended to exercise dominion/control over chattel
   a. See intent section
4. D interfered substantially
   a. Substantial change of character of the chattel

*P regains the chattel and is given the value of harm OR relinquishes the chattel to D for fair market value

PRIVILEGE & CONSENT

Privilege

- Action is normally prohibited, but circumstantially permitted
- Affirmative defenses > D bears burden of proof > "even assuming"
- P expected to prove lack of consent
- self-defense

Consent

- Explicit actual (writing, words, event inaction!) v. implied-in-fact (actual behavior)
- Volenti non fit injura: to one who consents, no wrong is done
- Could be communicated OR state of mind

    - Reasonably understood by those involved
- Honor Codes & Blood Feuds
    - Bengals: in sports there is a code, but when does the consent stop?
- Types:
    - Actual: state of mind
    - Informed: (1) duty to inform, (2) causation, (3) injury
    - Reasonably Apparent: reasonable person in actors shoes would think they consented
    - Substitute
    - Implied-in-law/constructive: unconscious and would consent to x
    - Emergency: public good

Invalidations

1. Invalidation by Fraud
    a. Consent to the particular conduct OR substantially same conduct
    b. Elements
        i. Induced to consent
            1. Aka there was consent but with actual knowledge would have made another decision
        ii. Substantial mistake or extent of harm to be expected
            1. The other knew there would be harm or that there was a mistake
            2. Over is no, under is fine
        iii. Mistake known by other OR induced by others' misrepresentation
            1. Purposeful or substantial assumption
            2. Doctor who falsely represented a friend for assistant
    c. Medical malpractice/ battery: when another doctor steps in
2. Under Duress

a. Spectrum:

Relationship Threat	Economic Threat	Physical Threat
• I'll never speak to your again, or never have sex with you again *Most likely won't count*	• Fire you • Prevent a raise *Most likely won't count if not substantial/only income* *Most likely will count if this affects the liveli-hood of the person*	• Kill you • Holding hand over gun holster *Most likely will count*

3. Lack of Capacity
    a. Actual, voluntary consent revoked when made by:
        i. temporary/permanent diminished mental ability
        ii. Minors
        iii. Intoxicated persons

Reasonable Patient (community test)

- alternatives/reasonably foreseeable risks & benefits
- Non-emergency or diagnostic only
- Reasonably prudent person would have chosen otherwise

DEFENSES

Self Defense *Personal Torts Only*

1. D believes there will be harmful or offensive contact
    a. Actual contact or imminent apprehension
2. D's belief is reasonable
    a. If the person starts it, cannot claim self-defense 2nd time around
    b. Fake gun: if knew compared to assumed real
3. D's force is reasonable
    a. Not likely to cause death/serious injury

b. Aka dont bring a gun to a fist fight

Defense of Others *Personal Torts Only*

1. D believes the 3rd person has a privilege of self-defense, & their action is necessary for the other's protection
2. D's belief is correct or reasonable
    a. Can't just step in the middle of a fight that we don't know who is causing what
    b. Even if wrong, as long as reasonable to believe, still ok
3. D's force is reasonable
    a. Proportionate to threat

Defense of Property *Personal Torts Only*

1. Intrusion on property can only be prevented/terminated by use of force
2. Belief is reasonable
3. Intrusion was unprivileged
    a. consent
4. Asked to desist or reasonable to believe the request would be useless
    a. Don't necessarily have to ask
5. Force was reasonable and not likely to cause death or serious harm
    a. Mere trespass against property other than a dwelling is NOT good enough to justify deadly weapon!

Recovery of Chattel

1. The other person tortiously took chattel
2. P had Immediate possession of chattel
    a. Not ownership necessary, for example, borrowing a car
3. P promptly went after chattel
    a. Not 1 hour later, must be immediate
4. Asked to return chattel or reasonable belief the request would be useless

a. If running away, don't have to ask

5. Force was reasonable and not likely to cause death or serious harm
   a. Mere tortiously taking an item is NOT good enough to justify deadly weapon!

Legal Authority

- Public Officials within scope of roles
- Reasonable limits
- Key Questions:
  a. Within jurisdiction/ authority of action
  b Probable cause/warrant
  c. Good faith
  d. Reasonable

Disciplining Children

- Reasonability:
  - Seriousness of offense
  - Past attitude and behavior of child
  - Availability of less severe or equally effective discipline
- Force to subdue v. force to punish
- One size does not fit all
- Babysitters CANNOT use this defense
- Teachers CAN use this defense
- Nannies... depend on the situation

Private Necessity *Property Torts Only*

- D may act in a way that would otherwise be trespass to chattel or conversion if:
  - Believed it was reasonable and necessary to protect from serious harm
  - Belief was reasonable
- Hypo 1: bear in woods and needed to get out of bear's way/ broke into cabin

- Hypo 2: tying boat to dock in storm/hurts the dock
- Liable for all damages, but privileged to take these actions

Public Necessity *Property Torts Only*

- D may act in a way that would otherwise be trespass to chattel or conversation if:
  - Act is reasonably believed to happen
  - Reasonably appear to be imminent
  - Completed in a reasonable manner
  - No unnecessary damage is made
- Not liable for any necessary damages
  - For example, when disassembling a bomb in hotel room—not liable for breaking down the door or damage to carpet from chemicals to dissolve bomb, yes liable if then a glass cabinet was shattered during celebration dance afterwards

NEGLIGENCE

- Elements:
  1. Duty: D has duty to act
  2. Breach of Duty: D failed to act
  3. Cause-in-Fact: D's act caused harm (actual cause)
  4. Proximate Cause: Untold/unforeseeable consequences
  5. Harm: P suffers actual, tangible harm (damages)
- Handled in 1 of 2 ways:
  - Jury: decision
  - Trial Judge: reasonable persons cannot differ
- Learned Hand Test
  - B < PL
  - Burden is less than Probability + Magnitude of Injury
- Questions to ask:
  - Was D negligent?
  - Is the negligence actionable?
  - *Both answers MUST be yes!*

- *No harm = no foul!*

Standard of Care (duty)

- What does duty entail?
  - Act with reasonable care to not cause harm to others
  - Those in "zone of danger"
- Whom is duty owed?
  - Those foreseeably at risk from D's conduct
- Reasonable person
- Must make home safe for guests—even just a warning can be OK sometimes
- Must have an established relationship

Breach

- When d acted unreasonably
- Jury determines:
  - Which facts are true AND
  - Whether, given those facts, D acted with reasonable care

Reasonable Person

- Facts matter
- 5 Paradoxes:
  - Uses caution such as a man of ordinary prudence would observe
  - Cannot use substandard skills or knowledge as an excuse
  - Is held responsible for specialized skills/kowledge they may have
  - May act differently in an emergency
  - Usually follows customary practice, but may sometimes be reasonable to not do so AND it may sometimes be unreasonable to do so
- Vaughn v. Menlove: hayrick, spontaneous combustion [PARADOX 1]

- Bonafide v reasonable caution: vague, subjective, precedent, systemic, jury
- Best to their judgement

- General Qualities and habits if human beings or community customs [PARADOX 2]
  - Younger children = greater care
- Declair v McAdoo, extraordinary care [PARADOX 3]
  - Tire blew, should have known
  - Doesnt matter low IQ, there is a reasonable assumption
  - If high IQ, held to higher standard
- Emergencies [PARADOX 4]
  - Cordas v Deealess Trans Co: emergency calculated, but not overriding
  - Split on whether juries should be given "emergency instruction" (majority favor)
  - Hargrive v McGinley: car hit right in front
  - Hypo: Crossing guard with gun shot
  - Constituting an Emergency:
    - Weather could count (Herr v Wheeler)
    - Sudden loss of consciousness of driver: no (underwood v knight)
    - Prior negligence: no (killing parents to go to orphan picnic, posas v hortan)
- Customary Practice [PARADOX 5]
  - Trimarco v Klein: entire industry is unlikely but can be negligent (no radios on tug boats)
  - Reasonable prudence = common prudence
    - Compliance to custom relevant but not binding
- Physical/Mental Attributes of Reasonable Person (Roberts v State of Louisiana)
  - Physical: same age, and other identifiers
  - Mental:

- Not providing exception for injuries caused by sudden onsent of mental illness w/o prior notice
- Belief: mental incapacity is never sudden, purpose is to compensate victim, not punish the tortfeasor!

◦ Contributory fault: courts are split

◦ Religious Beliefs
  - Is belief reasonable within context of that religion?
    - Overturned! Subjective views only (risk-utility balancing)

Judicially Determined Standards of Care

1. Courts utilizing risk-utility balancing to decide cases as a matter of law (jury)
   a. Resolve factual conflicts
   b. Set legal standard of reasonable care under circumstances

Think about whether it would place in more danger to do so!

2. Negligent per se
   a. An actor is negligent is, w/o excuse, they violate a statute that is designed to protect against the type of accident that actor's conduct causes, and if the statute is designed to protect (Martin v. Herzog)
   b. Violation of statute as presumption of negligence, prima facie: rubutted by proof a reasonable person would do the same thing (Reque v Milwaukee)
   c. Licensing: failure to obtain a license is not neg. Per se bc it is the missing SKILLS NOT LICENSE that caused the issue
   d. Overcompliance: statutes are usually minimum standards of class that do not provide for all contingencies (50MPH in snowstorm…)
3. Statutory Private Rights of Action: Express of Implied
   a. Consumer product safety act
      i. Injury by reason of knowing
      ii. Violation of consumer product safety rule

iii. Shall recover damages sustained

b. Federal crime statute

i. P must be member of class who specific benefit was enacted

ii. Indication of legislative intent to create private right of action

iii. Private right of action consistent with underlying purpose of statute

iv. P's cause of action must be not traditionally relegated to state law

Standard Conduct Child is Held

- Stevens v Veenstra
- Restatement 3rd: conform to the reasonably careful person of the same age, intelligence, and experience except less than 5 yrs old or adult activity
- Illinois Rule (rule of 7s)
    - <7: not negligent
    - 7-14: incapable of adult standards

2) Special Rules Limiting Possessors' liability

A) Firefighters rule

a) Firefighters or police who enter on premises of another to perform their functions were treated as licensees

b) Possessor of land owed no duty to make the premises safe nor to inspect for dangers unknown to possessor

c) *Pinter v. American Family Mutual Insurance*: firefighter was P who suffered injuries b/c of Ds negligence—court held "it offends public policy to say that a citizen invites private liability merely bc he happens to create a need for those public services"

d) Public servants do not assume the risk of every possible harm that might result from performance of their duties

i) Neg other than that which causes the need to intervention by P in the first place may be considered outside the risk assumed in accepting employment and be recoverable

B) Recreational-use statutes
   a) Partially immunize owner for accidents that take place on the property to help incentivize opening property to public
   b) NOT for people who charge money to use land
   c) This sometimes supersedes protection given to child trespassers

3) Duties Owed to those outside the premises
   A) Baseballs outside a stadium—still counts
   B) Water from gutter onto street—still counts
   C) Snow melting—doesnt count
   D) Artificial v. natural distinction
      a) Artificial: yes
      b) Natural: commercial user—reasonable care, other—duty only if risk is known or obvious
4) Duties Owned by Lessors
   A) Standard of reasonable care (unless common law where it was nonexistent, but most have scrapped due to so many exceptions)
   B) Sargent v. Ross Brief
5) Premises Liability: Securing Against Crime
   A) Reasonable security to prevent crime
      a) Posecai v. Walmart Stores, Inc

Foreseeability issue resolution:

1) Specific harm rule: landowner does not owe a duty to protect patrons from the violent acts of third parties unless he is aware of specific, imminent harm about to befall them
2) Prior similar incidents test: foreseeability is established by evidence of previous crimes on or near the premises
3) Totality of the circumstances tes (most common!): nature, condition, and location of the land, as well as any other factual circumstances bearing on foreseeability

4) Balancing test: address the interests of both business proprietors and their customers by balancing the foreseeability of harm against the burden of imposing a duty to protect against the criminal acts of third persons/ foreseeability of harm and gravity of harm must be balanced against the commensurate burden imposed on the business to protect against that harm

---

Kline

- breaches in security were so blatant that the causal relationship between the lax security and the attack on the P was well established

AKA Security gap is hard to define who takes responsibility

Vocab	**Definition**
Summary Judgment	Court order that no factual issues ramine to be tried (based on motion
De novo	Try the case "anew"
Prima facie case	Seems "open and shut"
Exemplary damages	Punitive, requested when D's acts were malicious, violent oppressive fraudulent, [grossly negligent], or grossly reckless
Vicarious liability	Imputed, attachment of responsibility from 1 person to another (group of crooks where only 1 kills someone, but they're all held responsible)
tort	wrong/injustice
Volenti non fit injuria	To one who consents, no wrong is done

Criminal Law Affirmative Defenses: Sample A

a) Justification—Focuses on the act, while it is illegal, the conduct was aimed at achieving social good. Burden of Proof—Prosecution must disprove; third parties can assist without criminal liability
   i) Self-Defense—Self-Defense Elements (605)—D had honest and reasonable belief: imminent threat, necessity to repel threat, proportional force (mistaken belief acceptable). Each element is a question for the fact-finding jury, and if all elements are met it's a complete defense and there's no criminal liability:
      1) Duty to Retreat
         a) Traditional—D not justified in using force in self-defense if D could flee safely or D was aware of the possibility
         b) Stand Your Ground Laws—majority, no duty to flee
      2) D is not the aggressor
         a) Exceptions:
            i) D was a non-deadly aggressor and the other party responded with an unexpected use of deadly force (then D regains the right to use self-defense)
            ii) D withdrew after their initial aggression and the other party continued to attack (must be verbally communicated and honest/authentic, but D does not have to run away or retreat)
      3) D was faced with a threat of imminent (presently occurring, about to occur without delay) unlawful force (force that is not privileged, ex: V grabs/points gun at D to steal D's personal property) (Generally speaking: words are not enough) (past (i.e. retaliation) or threat of future harm is insufficient). Exception: If someone is talking about future harm, but presently is waiving a gun at you then it is an imminent threat (essay only). Must be unlawful, if D is robbing and V responds with

non-deadly force, V is lawfully using force to repel D and D is not privileged to use SD

4) D's use of force was proportional to the perceived imminent harm (D cannot use excessive force).
   a) Non-deadly: allowed when used to resist any unlawful force
   b) Deadly: allowed where necessary to prevent immediate SBI/death (ex: someone points a gun/knife at you). Some jurisdictions allow the use of deadly force to prevent a felony or to apprehend a felon
5) D's belief that the unlawful force was imminent was reasonable
   a) D must believe that unlawful force was imminent (deadly force: must believe threatened with SBI/ Death)
   b) Belief must be reasonably objective
      i) Reasonable mistake—the defense of self-defense is not void
      ii) Unreasonable mistake—Maj defense is void; minority—imperfect self-defense which reduces the grading of a crime but does not eliminate criminal culpability (ex: murder reduced to manslaughter)

ii) Defense of Others—Defense of Others (638) honest & reasonable belief imminent danger of death/SBI, necessary, and proportionate. Early common law: Act-at-Peril (only if third party had legally use force in self-defense & D came to the rescue at own peril, D had a particular relationship status with V) Most jurisdictions have done away with Act-At-Peril and relationship limitations

iii) Imperfect Self-Defense—escalate from non-deadly to deadly force (not proportional force); belief is unreasonable—traditional common law would be guilty of murder; in some jurisdictions it mitigates homicide from murder to voluntary manslaughter

iv) Defense of Habitation—(642) generally deadly force not permissible in defense of property, however, it is permissible if the occupant of a dwelling (one's castle).
  1) Early common law—deadly force justified where dweller reasonably believed it was necessary to prevent an imminent and unlawful entry into their dwelling (castle doctrine)
  2) Modern—
    a) 3 elements are required
      i) Intruder has to actually enter/be in the process of entering
      ii) Home must be occupied when the entry occurred (some jurisdictions recognize habitation to include occupancy at a hotel room, vehicle, tent)
      iii) D has to believed that intruder is there to commit crime of violence/injure occupants (murder, BARRK, etc)—belief must be reasonable

v) Defense of Property—Non-deadly force may be used when it is reasonably necessary to:
  1) Prevent imminent dispossession or destruction of property in D's possession
  2) Regain possession of the property immediately after dispossession
    a) Reasonable non-deadly force allowed if acting immediately
    b) If the taking/interference has been completed then the use of force to recover the property is not allowed (hot pursuit)

vi) Emergency Situation—If D is under extraordinary pressure or an extreme situation without reasonable escape (conduct may harm another person/property but never homicide)
  1) Necessity—(673) D commits an unlawful act (voluntarily) to avoid some great harm (dire situation)
    a) Common Law

i) Threat—D compelled by non-human event (not coercion by another human being); usually from natural (teleological) force of nature (including physiological forces: lack of sleep)

ii) Imminent injury to person/property—to D's person (does not need to be threat of SBI/death, non-serious bodily harm and property damage are sufficient)

1) Danger of injury is immediate, D has not time to do anything else

2) Death by lot (trolly will hit either school kids or grannies)

iii) No reasonable alternatives (no way out)

iv) D's act must prevent equal/more serious harm: lesser evil (somebody will die either way and have to make a split decision as to whom). Pure economic threat is not enough (ex: not enough money to buy food)

v) D has Clean Hands: D didn't create conditions of own dilemma; D didn't take advantage of a dangerous force of nature to commit crime

vi) Limitations: homicide, civil disobedience, economic need, unclean hands

b) MPC

i) Threat—broader than common law as it allows for self and others; no imminence requirement

ii) Harm avoided is greater than the harm caused

iii) No Clean Hands Required, but defense is not permitted if D brought about the situation through negligence or recklessness

iv) Homicide permitted

2) Duress—Well-founded fear generated by a threat from a human being of imminent serious bodily harm or death to the D (or sometimes a near relative), D had reasonable

escape but for compliance with demands and to which D did not expose himself to the threat.

a) D's fear is reasonable (unreasonably believed (i.e. threat is not well-grounded and fear is unreasonable = no duress)
    i) MPC: if a person of reasonable firmness would be coerced
b) Narrowly applied, threat must come from human being
c) Imminent—Future/vague/undefined harm is insufficient, must be present, imminent and impending. The person has to have capacity to effect/cause harm to be effected immediately (by self or proxy)
d) Serious bodily harm or death
    i) D must be V of a threat (express or implied) of deadly force (compelling compliance) (lesser threats are insufficient, ex: property damage, economic hardship, minor injury)
        1) Early common law—limited to threats to D
        2) Modern Common law—includes threats to D's relatives (some jurisdictions also recognize when D has a duty of care)
        3) MPC: no requirement as to who must be threatened (D can be coerced by threat of harm to a stranger)
        4) D has an opportunity to escape, but for compliance with the demands (only way to avoid death/SBI was to commit the crime)
e) Nearly all courts deny defense if D exposed self to threat (voluntarily placed self in situation where substantial probability that he will be subjected to duress) (i.e. associating with known dangerous people)

b) Excuses—Focuses on the actor, D's conduct was wrongful, but D shouldn't be punished because of D's personal state/

condition (personality). Burden of proof—D must prove; only the D gets the benefit of the excuse (not assisting third parties)

i) Insanity (698)—if D is legally insane at the time of his criminal act, no criminal liability will be imposed.

1) M'Naghten Test—D is relieved of criminal liability if at the time of the act, D suffered from a severe mental disease/defect and as a result D was unable to know the nature/quality of their act or what D was doing was wrong. (focuses on D's reasoning abilities). D is relieved of criminal liability if at the time of the act, D suffered from a severe mental disease or defect and as a result D was unable to know:

a) D didn't know what he was doing (didn't understand the nature/quality of his act) OR

b) D didn't know what he was doing was wrong (had no ability to consider moral issues relevant to his behavior) (examples of did know it was wrong: trying to be covert, trying to escape without being seen, hiding, etc)

c) If D develops the mental defect after the act, then still culpable. If D recovers from the mental defect after the act, then relieved of criminal liability

2) Irresistible Impulse Test—As the result of a severe mental disease/defect, D is unable to control the impulse to commit the unlawful act/crime, and D thus comimits the unlawful act as a result

3) MPC Test—As a result of mental disease or defect, D lacks substantial capacity to either appreciate the criminality wrongfulness of his conduct OR conform his conduct to the requirements of the law (MPC broadened the M'Naghten test)

4) Durham Rule (Product Rule)—D is not "criminally responsible if his unlawful act is the product of a mental disease or defect." The Durham Rule was originally seen

as a way of simplifying the M'Naghten Rule and the Irresistible Impulse Test by making **insanity** and its relation to the **crime** a matter of objective diagnosis, but does not require a diagnosis of medical illness or disorder.

5) Federal Statutory Rule—at the time of the commission of the acts constituting the offense, the defendant, as a result of a severe mental disease or defect, was unable to appreciate the nature and quality or the wrongfulness of his acts.
6) 3 stages: At the time of the act, competency to stand trial, and death row (cruel and unusual punishment to execute criminally insane)

ii) Diminished Capacity Diminished capacity (729)
  1) Mens rea variant (case in chief)
  b) Partial responsibility variant
    a) A jury can acquit of charged offense and find guilty of lesser offense

iii) Infancy

iv) Intoxication (can also be a case in chief defense for specific crimes—negates mens rea)

Template Sample

Template

Self Defense

Self defense is an affirmative defense the defendant can assert when the D was faced with a threat of imminent, unlawful force, the use of D's force was necessary to repel the threat, the force used was proportional to the perceived imminent harm, and the D's belief that the unlawful force was imminent was reasonable. Generally, the defendant cannot be the aggressor.

There are two exceptions recognized to the prohibition that the D cannot be the aggressor. First, the D was a non-deadly aggressor and the other party responded with an unexpected use of deadly force (then D regains the right to use self-defense) or second, the D withdrew after their initial aggression and the other party continued to attack.

A threat is imminent if it is presently occurring or about to occur without delay. A future threat of harm is insufficient to establish this element. Unlawful force is force that is not privileged. Privileged force can stem from the V's own legal defenses as is the case when engaging in self-defense against an initial aggressor.

The force used by the D must be proportional to the threat of harm. Non-deadly force is permissible to resist any unlawful force whereas deadly force is only permissible when it is necessary to prevent immediate death or immediate serious bodily injury.

> A defendant that uses disproportionate force (escalates from non-deadly force to deadly force) is not able to assert self-defense, but may assert imperfect self defense. Imperfect self defense is not a complete defense, but rather under which the grading of the crime may be reduced.

The D must believe that unlawful force was imminent. To exercise deadly force, the D must believe that they were threatened with death or serious bodily injury. In either case, this belief must be objectively reasonable. This objective standard is based upon what a reasonable person would have done in the defendant's position, taking into consideration the background knowledge available to the D at the time. (Goetz) If the D was mistaken in their belief, but the mistake was reasonable the D is still able to escape culpability under self defense. However, in most jurisdictions, if the mistake was unreasonable the defense is void. A minority of jurisdictions recognize unreasonable mistakes as imperfect self-defense which will reduce the grading of a crime, but not absolve the D of criminal culpability entirely.

Traditionally the D was not justified in using force in self-defense if they were able to flee and aware of the possibility of doing so. The majority has instituted stand your ground laws under which there is no duty to flee.

Each element is a question for the fact finding jury, and if all elements are satisfied self-defense is a complete defense under which there is no criminal liability.

Defense of Others

A defendant can assert the affirmative defense, defense of others, when the D is intervened for a third party that was faced with a threat of imminent, unlawful force, the use of D's force was necessary to repel the threat, the force used was proportional to the perceived imminent harm, and the D's belief that the unlawful force was imminent was reasonable. At early common law, the D acted-at-peril, meaning the availability of this defense hinged on whether the V (limited to an individual with whom the D had a particular relationship status) had legal standing to self-defense. Most jurisdictions no longer impose act-at-peril or relationship limitations.

A threat is imminent if it is presently occurring or about to occur without delay. A future threat of harm is insufficient to establish this element. Unlawful force is force that is not privileged. Privileged force can stem from the V's own legal defenses as is the case when engaging in self-defense against an initial aggressor.

The force used by the D must be proportional to the threat of harm. Non-deadly force is permissible to resist any unlawful force whereas deadly force is only permissible when it is necessary to prevent immediate death or immediate serious bodily injury.

The D must believe that unlawful force was imminent. To exercise deadly force, the D must believe that they were threatened with death or serious bodily injury. In either case, this belief must be objectively reasonable. This objective standard is based upon what a reasonable person would have done in the defendant's position, taking into consideration the background knowledge available to the D at the time. (Goetz) If the D was mistaken in their belief, but the mistake was reasonable the D is still able to escape culpability under defense of others.

Each element is a question for the fact finding jury, and if all elements are satisfied self-defense is a complete defense under which there is no criminal liability.

Defense of Habitation:

Generally, deadly force was not permissible in defense of property, however, it is permissible to protect the occupants of a dwelling (one's castle). Under early common law, deadly force was justified where dweller reasonably believed it was necessary to prevent an imminent and unlawful entry into their dwelling (castle doctrine). Under modern common law, the intruder has to actually enter or be in the process of entering, the habitation must be occupied when the entry occurred (some jurisdictions recognize habitation more broadly than just a home); and the D has to believed that intruder is there to commit crime of violence or to injure occupants. The D's belief must be objectively reasonable. This objective standard is based upon what a reasonable person would have done in the defendant's position, taking into consideration the background knowledge available to the D at the time. (Goetz) If the D was mistaken in their belief, but the mistake was reasonable the D is still able to escape culpability under defense of others.

Defense of Property:

Non-deadly force may be used when it is reasonably necessary to prevent imminent dispossession or destruction of property in D's possession or to regain possession of the property immediately after dispossession. It is never permissible to use deadly force in protection of property, however, reasonable non-deadly force is protected if acting immediately following dispossession (acting in hot pursuit). However, if the taking/interference has been completed then the use of force, even non-deadly force, to recover the property is not allowed.

Necessity:

An emergency situation arises when the D is under extraordinary pressure or an extreme situation without reasonable escape. (non-human forces)

Duress:

An emergency situation arises when the D is under extraordinary pressure or an extreme situation without reasonable escape. Accordingly, the D may be in a state of duress, a well founded fear generated by a threat from a human being of imminent bodily harm or death to the D (or sometimes a near relative), D had a reasonable escape but for compliance with demands, and D did not exposed himself to the threat. Under this defense, a defendant may be absolved of criminal liability for harm to a person or property, but it will not excuse homicide.

D's fear is reasonable. If the threat is unreasonably believed either due to the threat not being well grounded or the fear is unreasonable, then the defense of duress will not apply. The MPC recognizes reasonableness if a person of reasonable firmness would be coerced.

This threat is narrowly applied and must come from a human being.

A threat is imminent if it is present or impending. A future threat of harm, a vague threat, or an undefined threat is insufficient to establish this element. The person making the threat must have capacity to immediately effect the harm, either on his own or via a proxy.

The D must be the V of an express or implied threat of deadly force that compelled the D's compliance. Threats of a lower severity than deadly force are insufficient. Under early common law the threats were limited to those directly against the D. Modern Common law expanded to include threats to D's relatives, with some jurisdictions also recognizing those to whom D owes a duty of care. The MPC is the most broad as there is no limitations as to whom the threat is made against, even a D responding to the threat of harm to a stranger is sufficient.

If the D has an opportunity to escape, but for compliance with the demands. The only way for the D to avoid death or serious bodily injury was to commit the crime.

Nearly all courts deny the defense if D exposed himself to the threat by voluntarily placing himself in situation where there was a substantial probability that he would be subjected to the duress.

Excuses:

Insanity—M'Naghten Test: If a D is legally insane at the time of his criminal act, no criminal liability will be imposed and instead the D will be committed for psychiatric oversight. The courts use a number of tests to evaluate whether or not the D was legally insane at the time of the act, including the M'Naghten test. Under the M'Nagten test, a D is relieved of criminal liability if at the time of the act, D suffered from a severe mental disease or defect and as a result D was unable to know what he was doing (didn't understand the nature/quality of his act) or the D didn't know what he was doing was wrong (had no ability to consider moral issues relevant to his behavior).

If D develops the mental defect after the act, then the D is still culpable. If D recovers from the mental defect after the act, then the D is still relieved of criminal liability

Criminal Law Affirmative Defenses: Sample B

Case in Chief

- Poking holes
- Include in elemental analysis

Affirmative

- Analyze after determined whether all elements will be met
- Burden of proof
    - Justification: examine circumstances at time act was committed, focuses on offense, sports principle valued by society
        - Law tends to require prosecution to disprove
        - Self d, d of others, d of habitation, d of property, necessity
    - Excuse
        - Defense has to prove
        - Insanity, diminished capacity, infancy, intoxication

Emergency Situation

- Extraordinary pressure/extreme situation
- Does reasonable escape
- Conduct harms another person/property

Property II Case Log: Sample

Drake	Broker entitled to commision when ready, able, willing buyer per seller's terms	majority
Dobbs	absent seller's default, broker due commission when sale is consummated	minority
Curtis	partial performance of oral modified contract removes from SOF	
Donovan	American Rule: if S defaults, B gets compensatory damages (replaced old English rule that only allowed restitution)	
Schwinder	specific performance on condo made unique by improvements	
Orr	liquidated damages clause enforced when P retained deposit (P can't also go after damages)	
Miller	when time of essence clause isn't included, either party is entitled to reasonable adjournment of the closing date	
Lape	line of sight easement was an unmarketable title	
Grant	Can waive contingency clause if it only benefits that party (jurisdictional split on judgment liens: junior line prevail or equitable title)	
Bale	deed affective when placed in control of grantee with grantor's present intent to convey, changes made to a deed after delivery have no affect	minority also req. acceptance
Ward	If no access to the deed, it is not a present intent to convey	
Wiggill	a future conveyance does not meet the element of present intent to convey	
Strambovsky	financial benefit from ghost rumors, so must disclose even though in jurisdiction that would otherwise not require it	

Jensen	Disclosure requires buyer's actual knowledge, imputed knowledge (i.e. constructive) is not sufficient	
Speight	Remote purchase in breach of warranty of workman like construction	split on remote purchaser
Brown	Future covenants are only breached on eviction, not merely on learning of a superior property interest	
Dover	CL a lease prior to mortgage survives, but a junior lease entered into after mortgage is extinguished on foreclosure	
Millette	interest perfected on recordation against all third parties (majority), rather than following the minority view of requiring an additional step of enforcement	

▷▷▷ APPENDIX C

Practice Hypotheticals

The best way to learn the law is to apply what you have learned to a variety of hypothetical situations. Of course, you can always create your own or download some from the internet. We have also provided a few of our own to get you started. We recommend treating these as essay prompts, but at the minimum, use them to issue spot and outline key points to cover.

Civil Procedure

Question 1. Tristan and Kara were in a car accident in Massachusetts. Tristan moves to New York for college, and despite saying he intends to stay in New York after college, Tristan does not change his driver's license, doctors' offices, or mailing address. Tristan sues for $75,000 in damages. Tristan serves Kara for a tort action for negligence in federal court while Kara is at a job interview in New York. Does the court have subject matter jurisdiction and personal jurisdiction? Did Kara receive proper notice?

Question 2. Karen, from South Dakota, sues Big Book and Print World for $50,000 for copyright infringement in South Dakota state court. Big Book is incorporated in and with its principal place of business in South Dakota. Print World is incorporated in Delaware and has its principal place of business in Minnesota. Print World removes the case to federal court. Is removal proper?

Constitutional Law

Question 1. The United States Federal Government has instituted a marshmallow tax. They have completed studies that show the making and consumption of marshmallows in the aggregate is dangerous to both the environment and human health. This tax is meant to deter companies from making as much marshmallow as they made previously. The tax would be applied threefold: (1) 50% tax to any company who makes marshmallows, (2) $300 tax to any individual being who has marshmallows on their person when they are on government property (no matter the amount), and (3) 90% tax on any marshmallows sold across state lines. Analyze each of the taxes and regulations and determine which, if any, are constitutional, and explain your answer for each.

Question 2. Todrick is the leader of a local religious sect that uses specialty soap for religious ceremonies, infused with glitter. These soaps are an integral part of the religion, and it is well-recognized that people are covered with this specialty glitter when they have completed specific ceremonies.

The city Todrick's religious sect sits in is hosting a city-wide celebration of recent renovations downtown. Todrick has offered to donate enough of the specialty soap to make the local lake a sparkly hot spot for participants, as well as to double for anyone who wishes to partake in a ceremony of the faith. The city would love to have a place where more of the younger population would want to congregate for selfies to get them involved, and a sparkly lake would do just that. However, this will require a lot of long-term clean up on behalf of the city since glitter does not just "disappear" after a ceremony or celebration. If the city accepts Todrick's donation, will it have violated the Establishment Clause? Why or why not?

Contracts

Question 1. Ty'shawn holds homeowners insurance with HousesCertfied, a well-known insurance company. The policy covers a range of unfortunate events, but requires proper notice and filing to grant coverage. Sadly, three years into his coverage, Ty'shawn's home experiences catastrophic flooding. Flooding is covered by his policy so long as it is reported within four days. Ty'shawn calls the company on the third day because his home is so flooded he cannot even get in to take pictures, as required by the company. HousesCertified's agent says the company automatically applies an extra day if the final day is a nationally recognized holiday. The fourth day lands on Sweetest Day, but Ty'shawn does not personally celebrate this holiday. Trying his luck, Ty'shawn submits his request for coverage 5 days after the flooding occurred and is denied. Which party is most likely to succeed and why?

Question 2. Tickle Me Pink Fencing (TMPF) company entered into a contract with Berry S. Weet to paint all of the fence surrounding his house a bubblegum pink. The contracts outlined that for $5000, paid upon completion, TMPF would use a pink paint that was actually color-matched with the most well-known gum brand. TMPF would start February 1st and be completed by February 13th.

TMPF does finish painting in the early hours of February 14th, about 9am. However, the delay was caused by distributor paint delays, which meant they were one shade away from the initially promised color. To an untrained eye, the color still looked the same. Both paints cost the same. TMPF was the most concerned about completing the fence for Berry S. Weet's in-home business opening on February 14th, and it would have cost over $10,000 to rush order the exact paint color in time.

Explain what remedies might exist for Berry S. Weet as well as what rights and liabilities Tickle Me Pink Fencing might have and why.

Criminal Law

Question 1. Larry had been watching Jerry's home for weeks. Larry knew that Jerry's toaster was really a portal to another world. Larry devised a plan to sneak in at night and steal Jerry's toaster. Larry prepared for his mission dutifully, bringing along his trusty black balloon sword. Jerry heard noise in the kitchen and grabbed his pocket knife. When Jerry entered the dark kitchen, Jerry saw Larry standing there wielding a funny looking sword and clutching his toaster. Larry panicked and threw the toaster at Jerry's head. Jerry fell back, striking his head on the kitchen counter. Larry fled the scene and Jerry died from his injuries. What are the charges the prosecution would assert and what defenses would Larry assert?

Real Property

Question 1. Ally inherits the northeast quarter of her grandfather's land, while Bobby inherits all the other quarters of the land. Ally is terrible at directions, and mistakenly believes the piece she inherits contains the cabin in the woods, which is actually in Bobby's land in the northwest corner of the section. Ally takes up residence, and Bobby knows she is living on the land. Ally maintains half the land in the northwest quarter, up to an established fence line. Bobby never talks to Ally about her living in the cabin, but he doesn't mind since he is using Ally's land to graze his cattle herd, as well as the portion of the northwest quarter not being maintained by Ally. After 25 years, Ally's lawyer, while writing her will, realizes she has been living on the wrong section of land. Ally brings an action to quiet the title to the land and Bobby counters. Who owns what land?

Question 2. Bank has a lease for office space with Landlord for five years, with an annual rent due January 1st of $24,000. When the lease was renewed, Landlord and Bank did not sign a new lease, but verbally agreed to continue under the old lease's current terms. Landlord dies one year into the "new lease" and Son takes ownership. Son does not want Bank as a tenant anymore. What type of lease do the Bank and Son have, and how can the Son terminate the lease?

Torts

Question 1. Karl and Ben are at a private gun range. To be a member, everyone must go through a safety orientation of the rules before being given access to the range. Karl was shooting at one side of the range. When he finished, he turned on the red range indicator light and went down range to adjust his target. While Karl was down range, Ben entered the range, ignored the light, and began firing at the farthest firing point from Karl's firing point (about 30 feet). Karl yelled "You idiot! I am going to kill you!" and headed back up the range, staying in his firing line. When he reached his firing point, Karl picked up his gun and equipment and walked towards Ben to exit the range. The whole way out the range, Karl continued to swear, call Ben names, and make violent comments such as "someone needs to knock some sense into you." What torts have been committed?

Question 2. Craig has closed his business and decided to go to a car dealership to look at new cars. The salesman offers to look at Craig's van to determine the trade-in value, and Craig gives him his keys while he goes for a test drive.

(A) When Craig comes back, the salesman refuses to return his keys because another customer wants to buy Craig's van. After arguing with the staff for two hours, Craig calls the police, at which time the dealership returns his keys. Have any torts been committed?

(B) When Craig comes back, the dealership has sold Craig's van to another customer, and the customer has taken the vehicle off the lot after signing what he believed was a completed purchase and sale agreement. Craig is stuck at the dealership for six hours before he is able to return home. Craig is forced to buy a new vehicle. Six months later the van is returned to him, after being driven over 50,000 miles and with significant damage. Does Craig have any claims against the customer? Does Craig have any claims against the dealership?

▷▷▷ APPENDIX D

School Supply Lists

Law school comes with a book list, but probably not a general supply list. You will obviously want the required textbooks, as well as a laptop that will meet your school's requirements. But what else will you need? Here are our personal curated lists of school supplies, as well as some supplemental items to always keep on hand.

Jessica's School Supply List

- A blue light screen protector or glasses—get this early! It will save you headaches down the road, literally.
- Highlighters in assorted colors—I prefer the thinner ones, that are roughly the same thickness as a pen.
- Pens—in your favorite style.
- Sticky flags—to mark off pages or cases.
- Three ring binders—I use them for everything: hard copies of the lecture slides, book print outs, notes, and organizing research papers.
- Divider tabs for binders—these are especially useful for organizing memos and dividing cases.
- Flashcards
- Notepads for scratch paper—write a to-do list, questions that pop into your head, or notes on an asynchronous question that you want to remember when it comes time to answer.
- A web camera—if your computer doesn't have one built in, this is a necessity. If it does have it built in, your school may suggest you

have one in case your camera fails during an exam since often cameras are required during proctored exams.

- Headache medicine—you will inevitably get a few headaches, whether it's too much screen time, poor posture, or stress. Make sure you don't overuse whatever medicine you choose, or mix it up to avoid long term side effects.
- A water bottle you actually like—whatever it takes to stay hydrated.
- Notebooks—I get two 1-subject notebooks per a class in the same color; 1 for case briefs, and 1 for actual note taking during class. I prefer to write almost everything by hand because I remember it better.

JESSICA'S TIP

You will likely be printing a lot more than you ever expected. From my experience laser printers tend to last longer and be cheaper in the long run. If you are using your work printer primarily, just remember that you will need to pre-plan what you need printed and you may not be able to print slides if a professor posts them only a few minutes before the start of class.

Bethany's School Supply List

- Notebooks—I get ones that are easily identifiable from one another so I can easily grab the correct subject. I have found taking notes physically on the first read through and then converting them to a Google Doc in shorthand helps best with my comprehension of the material.
- Pens & Highlighters—I like to find ones that are comfortable for my hand. I didn't mind a splurge here to make it more comfortable with hours of note taking.
- Laptop/Desktop—Personally I prefer to work on a large, dual monitor desktop when I am attending classes and completing work at home. However, the laptop allows me to take my work on the go when we have social commitments or I just get bored looking at the same four walls after too many hours working on a single brief.

- Agenda—I am very particular about a written agenda, but my preference is the cheap $10 version from Walmart. I supplement with stickers to make it personalized.
- Furniture—This was an initial expense, but well worth it. It included a foot rest, supportive chair, book stand strong enough for a law textbook, and large screen desktop.
- Paper/Printer/Ink—Prior to law school, I was fine reading things online. Now, if things are longer than three scrolls online, I prefer to print. It is way easier on the eyes!
- Accordion Folder—This is a great place to keep all of your printed materials for the semester, then empty it out and use it again the following semester.
- Essential Oils—I personally keep three blends on hand right next to my desk by DoTerra: Cheer, Motivate and Thinker.
- Pocket Supplements—These aren't a replacement for class notes, but very helpful to supplement the materials if you need clarification or can't think of a way to word something just right.

BETHANY'S TIP — x

You probably have most of what you need already available. I have pulled out old school supplies saved from many years prior (even as far back as high school) to use for law school. Obviously, I purchase a new agenda each year due to the date needs, but I pull out an old notebook with some paper left in it and use it until it's gone. Family members and friends might also have some old materials they no longer need or want and they make great gifts!

Sarah's School Supply List

- A high quality printer—I quickly found that being able to print things out, from memo editing to marking up cases, was an essential for me to succeed.
- Copy paper.
- Book tabs—I like to put a book tab at the start of each case in my text books. This helps me quickly jump to the case in my book during the lecture.

- Mechanical pencils—no time for sharpening mid-lecture, just click out more graphite and keep going!
- Looseleaf notebook paper.
- One binder per subject.
- Plastic dividers—I like to print my slides and put my notes for each lecture into its own section within my binder.
- Highlighters—I use these to make notes of case quotes I want to use in legal writing.
- Fine point pens of different colors—I use these to book brief. I always use green for the issue, red for the holding, blue for the rules, yellow for the analysis, and a different color for the dissent. This is a life saver during cold calls!
- Webcam. My laptop has a built-in webcam, but I like to have an extra one just in case something goes awry with my laptop heading into an exam. Honor code violation isn't on my bucket list, so I like having an extra one around just in case!
- One package of flashcards just in case, but I don't really use these and just buy them out of habit.
- Stapler and staples. I use maybe five staples per semester and it's usually when I am editing a paper.
- Chocolate and comfy slippers. These are essentials for me and it's OK for you to grab a couple of comfort items too!

SARAH'S TIP

I reuse my book tabs from week to week and my binders/plastic dividers semester to semester. Once a semester ends, I discard my barely sticky book tabs and put the contents from my binder onto the shelf with my outline on the top. Then I print my syllabus for the next semester and place it at the front of my binder, ready for the next round!

Index